PRAISE FOR *C.A.R.E.*

"Peter van Stralen knows that when you care about your team, they will pass along that caring attitude to your customers, and success will follow. If you haven't yet created a culture of care in your organization, read *C.A.R.E. Leadership* and make it happen."
>—Ken Blanchard, coauthor of *The One Minute Manager*®
>and *Trust Works*

"In a fast-paced world that changes at lightning speed, it is vitally important (and necessary) to be grounded in unchanging values and principles. Peter has revealed these timeless gifts in a simple, passionate, personal, powerful and inspiring story. Most of us feel these principles in our heart, conscience and spirit. *C.A.R.E. Leadership* reminds us that the business of enhancing lives enriches our own and helps us change the world in positive and long-lasting ways."
>—Tony DiGiovanni, executive director of *Landscape Ontario*

"*C.A.R.E. Leadership* will give you incredible insights into building a great organization. Peter van Stralen has proven that with Sunshine Brands. More importantly, he reminds us all as leaders that we must continually be learning and applying the wisdom that can be found all around us, if we only have the courage to look."
>—Jim Paluch, president of JP Horizons; author of *Leaving a Legacy*

"*C.A.R.E. Leadership* is an impressive and refreshing book. Peter van Stralen's journey of how he and his brothers have literally built The Grounds Guys business from the ground up is entertaining, informative, and inspiring. I particularly love the way he has crafted important principles of leadership into practical frameworks that can be immediately grasped and implemented. Peter writes with the conviction of someone who has truly put their ideas to the test. This is great stuff."
>—Greg Nathan, founder of the Franchise Relationships Institute

"Wow! What a great book! It isn't theory or philosophy but practical real-world leadership. I don't think I've read a book with so much practical, useable, trainable information packed into it."
>—Joel Worthington, vice president of operations, Mr. Electric

"There is much to admire about this work and a great deal that could be said to recommend its reading. At its essence, however, I would say this: If you are seeking both significance and success and realize that going to work every day for a dollar is the height of poverty thinking—then *C.A.R.E. Leadership* is for you."

—Jim Amos, chairman of Tasti D-Lite /Planet Smoothie; former CEO of Mail Boxes Etc.

"This book is a must-read for anyone in a leadership position. Whether you're an experienced leader looking for new perspective or a new leader looking for best practices, this is the book for you. The clarity and focus that Peter van Stralen brings to his thinking on how to be a great leader is refreshing, and his writing makes you feel like you're having a great chat over coffee. Your time will be well spent and your leadership will be reinvigorated."

—Lorraine McLachlan, president and CEO of the Canadian Franchise Association

"Having worked with Peter for several years, I already knew the story well—yet I couldn't put the book down. I read it from start to finish in one sitting. I never saw a company that didn't list customer service as their top priority, yet most companies struggle to deliver excellence at the very point where employees interact with customers. With *C.A.R.E. Leadership*, business owners inspire employees at every level to embrace and transmit the owner's passion for excellence down to the customers. It is this 'secret sauce' that has made The Grounds Guys an industry leader in landscape management."

—Ron Madera, president of The Grounds Guys USA

"*C.A.R.E. Leadership* is an engaging and insightful story of how one family used perseverance, passion, and mutual respect to build an amazing brand across North America. It is written through the eyes of the author's life experiences, much like a storybook. I felt like I was reading an entertaining autobiography, yet the story is chock-full of leadership lessons for the business and non-business reader alike. *C.A.R.E. Leadership* is a 'feel good' business book about doing it the right way—in business, at home, or in the community."

—Mike Bidwell, president and COO of The Dwyer Group

PETER VAN STRALEN

Foreword by Dina Dwyer-Owens

C.A.R.E.

LEADERSHIP

8 Principles That Will Transform the Culture of Your Business and Unleash the Full Potential of Your Team

Published by River Grove Books
Austin, Texas
www.greenleafbookgroup.com

Distributed by River Grove Books

For ordering information or special discounts for bulk purchases, please contact River Grove Books at PO Box 91869, Austin, TX 78709, 512.891.6100.

Design and composition by Greenleaf Book Group LLC
Cover design by Greenleaf Book Group LLC

Cataloging-in-Publication data
(Prepared by The Donohue Group, Inc.)

Van Stralen, Peter, 1969-
  C.A.R.E. leadership : 8 principles that will transform the culture of your business and unleash the full potential of your team / Peter van Stralen ; foreword by Dina Dwyer-Owens.—1st ed.
    p. : ill. ; cm.

  1. Corporate culture—Case studies. 2. Grounds Guys—Case studies. 3. Leadership—Case studies. 4. Customer service—Case studies. I. Dwyer-Owens, Dina. II. Title. III. Title: CARE leadership

HD58.7 .S77 2013
658.4   2013942439

Print ISBN: 978-1-938416-37-8
eBook ISBN: 978-1-938416-38-5

First Edition

Dedication

This book is dedicated to my beloved parents, Fred and Nellie van Stralen and my wonderful siblings, Monika, Julia, Tim, Erika, Deborah, Derek, Seth, James, Mark, Paul, Kristina, Ben, John, and Luke, who are the originators of the culture of CARE. I love all of you.

I also dedicate this book to our franchise partners and their teams, who are so passionate about our brands and who create a remarkable experience for our customers every day.

I dedicate this book to my home office team as well. Thank you, Scott Bryk, for your tremendous support on this project, and thanks to Michael McLaughlin, Erik Premont, Kaare Myrland, Frank Myrland, Joyce Stehouwer, and Katelyn Martin, who allowed me to articulate these concepts and bounce ideas off of them every day while writing this book.

And finally I dedicate this book to my best friend and wife, Carol, and our wonderful children, Caroline, Peter and Daniel. Thank you for your unconditional love and care, without which this book would have never been written.

Contents

I've met a lot of business leaders in my career. I've inked a lot of deals. I've been schooled in an education of learning by doing. And I've had the honor of navigating that journey with five brothers and sisters who grew up in a family business with me. Those lessons aren't common. But they are lessons that Peter van Stralen knows first-hand! I am sure that is why I instantly connected with Peter and the business now known as The Grounds Guys at our very first meeting.

Thanks to The Dwyer Group's president, Mike Bidwell, I received a great article about Peter's company. Here was an incredible story of hard work, family dedication, and entrepreneurial success. I have to admit, it sounded eerily familiar. But something of bigger value was at the heart of this business. Ah, yes, values! That's what resonated from the beginning, and it continues to be what separates an everyday business from a giant of the industry in my eyes.

I only knew Peter's business from afar at first. But once I saw how he and his brothers get along in managing that business, I knew the kind of first-class operation they were growing. That's because the love and respect the van Stralens showed for one another told me the kind of CARE they were giving their customers as well. And it's that CARE Leadership that you will read about in these pages, offering an approach to business that can make a difference in your life and your business as well.

Those measurable values have instilled a culture at The Grounds Guys and at Sunshine Brands in Canada that has fit perfectly with our Live R.I.C.H. culture at The Dwyer Group and the themes of Respect, Integrity, Customer focus, and Having fun in the process that permeate The Dwyer Group Code of Values, too. Peter gets it. He leads by example. He treats business like he treats his family: with love, a devotion to nurturing one another along, and an understanding that in giving we receive. In *C.A.R.E. Leadership*, Peter explains one of the most important lessons in business. It's not just about making money; it's about doing good, and The Grounds Guys are doing a great deal of good, thanks to the solid foundation the van Stralen Family has built. Their CARE Leadership approach is creating a wake of other CARE Leaders.

You may not come from a big family with fifteen kids and sixty grandkids. You may not have a mother and father who instilled the same work ethic. You may not even have a vision for your business or your life. But what you can do—what we all can do—is learn to CARE. And oh, what a great world this would be if more people learned to be CARE Leaders. As Peter shows in these pages, dreams can come true.

Lead with CARE,

Dina Dwyer-Owens

Chairwoman and CEO,

The Dwyer Group®

HOW WE GOT HERE

My mission is "to share the Culture of CARE™." For me this means that every day I have the opportunity to share with as many people as possible the values and principles of CARE Leadership, which have helped and continue to help us find success. This mission provides me with the inspiration and excitement I need to come to work every day equipped with an effective mindset. With this simple mission, I know each day WHAT I'm going to do, HOW I'm going to do it, and most importantly, WHY I'm doing it. No matter what my day throws at me, I'm ready to face it with passion and purpose. I didn't always have this much passion in my career, but along the way I was able to find my voice. This book is about how I found my inspiration and purpose, and I hope that my story can inspire you to find your voice and to create a culture that can help others to find theirs.

A CHANGING PARADIGM

We are operating in a new era of business today, moving out of the industrial age and into what Peter Drucker called the "Knowledge Worker Age":[1] an age defined by a generation of workers who are informed and connected with access to the same technology and information as their bosses. It is an age brought on by the free flow of information, changing demographics, and the proliferation of the Internet. Today almost every worker, whether upper management or laborer, carries in their hands the ability to communicate freely with the world through social media, along with access to all of the knowledge that was once exclusively the domain of the elite and scholarly.

The industrial age, with all of its faults, did bring about many great changes to the business world, such as process automation, efficiency, and mass production. The predominant mindset of managers in that era seemed to be one of exploitation of people for their labor resources with little if any regard for the individual. Workers, it seems, were seen as an annoying expense rather than a valuable asset. This era gave birth to some of the management techniques and philosophies that still exist in many businesses today, such as top-down management, where the people in positions of authority call all the shots and the laborers simply do what they are told. The motivation technique of that era is known as "carrot and stick," a form of manipulation where workers have the hope of a reward if they produce and the fear of punishment if they don't. GAAP principles used today are a remnant of that era, where people are listed on the P&L statement as an expense, but a big tractor or other machines are shown on the balance sheet as an asset. This seems so backwards in today's information-age economy.

---

1   Source: *Wikipedia* (http://en.wikipedia.org/wiki/Knowledge_worker). "These new knowledge workers value life-long learning over life-long employment" (Bogdanowitz and Bailey, 2002).

I call today's version of industrial-age thinking "the BOSS mentality™." The boss mentality does not produce happy, inspired, and engaged team members, and over time this situation begins to erode the productivity and profitability of an organization. The informed, mobile, Internet-savvy, connected workforce of today needs more than just a job that exploits physical capacities. Today's workforce needs to be seen and respected as people with souls, hearts, and minds, not just as "things" to be managed and ordered about. The BOSS mentality needs to give way to a new mindset that sees a team member as a whole person with unlimited potential. Inspired and engaged people are not an expense; they are in fact one of a business's only assets that, when nurtured and cared for, appreciate in value. This book is about a new mindset that I call CARE Leadership™. We will explore the underlying principles and philosophies of CARE Leadership that can be applied to any organization and that has helped us grow a small lawnmowing business into a multimillion dollar, multi-national franchise brand.

HOW TO GET THE MOST OUT OF THIS BOOK

I recommend reading this book all the way through to get an understanding of the subject matter and how each principle relates to the others. I recommend writing notes as you go. Writing down your thoughts and reflections helps you remember them, and these notes will be a great resource for you later, helping you and your team to internalize the CARE Leadership principles and integrate them into your organization's culture. You can also sign up at www.createacultureofcare.com for free videos and other helpful downloads related to the content of this book, and you can follow me on Twitter—@petervanstralen—for the latest updates. *In fact why not take a moment to connect with me on Twitter right now and let me know you are reading this book. I'd love to hear from you!*

Going forward, you and your team can read one of the principles each month. Spend the month implementing the practices associated with one of the principles before moving on to the next. Once a week, during a morning meeting, use the time to recite and eventually memorize the eight principles. Discuss and share amongst the team examples and opportunities from the previous day where one of the principles came into play and how it changed an outcome for the better. As you and your team deep-dive into these principles, you will begin to see measurable changes taking place in team dynamics and synergy as well as in productivity and performance.[2]

To make sure you fully understand CARE Leadership, I will begin by talking about my experiences growing up in a large family and reflect on the parallels between that family atmosphere and the business culture of our company. This culture is now known affectionately as the Culture of CARE™ and is the product of following the principles of CARE Leadership.

In articulating the eight principles, I saw how the leadership examples set by our parents, long before we started our business, became the foundation of the Culture of CARE. I often draw the comparison between a functional business and a functional family. In a functional family the children are fed and sheltered in an atmosphere of friendliness, security, and love. They are given correction, guidelines, curfews, and standards to uphold. They are taught skills and allowed to develop as individuals: learning first to crawl and then to walk, then being taught how to read, ride a bike, and eventually drive a car. Along the way they are allowed and encouraged to contribute meaningfully to the family by doing chores and other jobs so that

---

2   The eight CARE Leadership principles can be used internally at your organization when referenced with the following tag line: "Trademarked by Peter van Stralen; used with permission."

they can feel like a part of something greater than themselves. This nurturing and development of people rather than their exploitation is what CARE Leadership is all about.

WHERE IT ALL STARTED

I grew up in a family of seventeen people! My parents had ten sons and five daughters. In case you are wondering: yes, they were all single births, and yes, just one set of parents. I truly believe that much of our business success is attributable to the principle-based values instilled in us as children. We saw examples of these values lived out every day by our parents, so that by the time we started our business, we had a solid foundation on which to begin building.

My parents were exceptional communicators. My mom used to say, "No one in our family will ever end up in the nuthouse; we communicate too much for that." My parents knew that to be successful as a family we would need to make respectful and open communication a priority. They bought a huge oak dining room table, and every day we sat together to eat dinner and talk about our day. Mom would go around the table, asking each one of us how our day went at school. No one could choose not to participate; she was an expert listener and she knew how to get everyone involved. Whatever the worry was that you carried home from school that day, you left the dinner table with a weight lifted off your shoulders.

As a teacher, my dad was always learning. He was an interesting man to me as a kid growing up, and he still is. He was intellectually curious and took an interest in everything we were learning. Later when he joined us in the business, he brought that desire for learning with him and instilled in us a hunger to learn something new every day.

My parents knew their role as the leaders of the family and knew that they wanted to set the bar high. Even when times were tough they maintained a positive attitude. They knew that we all looked to them for guidance and that we were more likely to follow what we saw them do rather than what they said.

My parents understood that they couldn't watch over us all the time to police our behavior—there were simply too many of us. They also knew that if they helped us to understand the consequences of making bad decisions and the rewards of making good ones, then we would make the right decisions with or without them. They understood that if they had made all of the decisions for us and dictated our behavior, than we would become reliant on their presence. Children who are not taught discernment between good and bad, and who simply "comply" with the rules for fear of punishment, often fall flat on their face when they find themselves alone and faced with a serious crossroad. However, we were free to choose between right and wrong, and more often than not we made the right choices. Perhaps this was because our parents had painted such a vivid picture of the negative consequences associated with a wrong decision. If they sensed that we didn't have the maturity or desire to make the right choices, then they would step in to reinforce and uphold our family values. I can still hear my dad saying, "A good name is rather to be chosen than great riches . . ."[3] I knew that I surely wasn't going to be the one to soil the family name. I feel the same today about our brands.

~

When my brother Tim and I turned thirteen and twelve, we were old enough to go on a camping trip to Algonquin Park in North Ontario with our church youth group. It was scheduled at the end of the summer, and Dad said we could go, but first we needed to de-nail, cut, and

---

3   Proverbs 22:1

stack a large pile of scrap wood that was lying in the yard. We accepted the challenge and got right at it. This was a big pile of wood and we had our work cut out for us. I think my dad knew that if we endured and finished the job we would have a deep sense of accomplishment. He knew that we would be tested to the limits of our endurance, even to the point of tears, but we would learn to press on with the goal of the camping trip ahead of us. He was also instilling in us a solid work ethic. The woodpile became known as the Algonquin Pile, and eventually the "gonk pile." There were many times that summer when we wanted to quit, but we knew that if we did, we would be forfeiting our goal, so we soldiered on. Dad didn't have to push us; he simply asked from time to time how it was going and if we needed help in any way. He would remind us of our goal and encourage us to carry on. We finished the pile and went camping. It was an awesome trip. We were so proud of our accomplishment, and we learned the power of taking ownership of a project and of keeping our eye on the prize.

Running a large household is not unlike running a business, and we all learned the value of a hard-earned dollar. We all gladly contributed our pay from summer and evening jobs to help buy "bread," as we put it in those days. We learned that both saving and earning were important to make things work, and we helped contribute to both in whatever way we could. People often ask us, "How did your parents keep all fifteen of you fed? Did you have to go without from time to time?" Quite the contrary; due to the resourcefulness of my parents, we ate like kings! Not only that, but friends and neighbors who were often over to play sports or other activities regularly shared at our dinner table. That resourcefulness and skill of maximizing financial resources, while helping others is at the root of what we today call our "triple bottom line."

We used to travel quite a bit on road trips as kids to visit friends in places like Connecticut, Delaware, Ottawa, and Detroit. My dad had a big sixteen-seat van, and we'd all jump in and hit the road. I think it was on trips like this where we learned how to have and share an opinion, but not to complain if we got overruled. When it came time to choose what or where to eat, it would have been impossible to drive one kid to Taco Bell, another to KFC, and yet another over to McDonalds so we could all have what we wanted. The way Dad managed the situation was to announce, "We are stopping at McDonalds for a burger and a milkshake. Would you like chocolate, strawberry, or vanilla?"

This ability to compromise individual will for the good of the group put us in good stead for our futures in the franchising industry. To take an excerpt from our operations manual, "Franchising may be described as 'collective thought' rather than 'individual thought.' Franchising assumes that what is right or correct for the whole franchise system is, by extension, right for the collected individuals in that system."

My dad was a schoolteacher, but as his family grew he opted to take a job as a letter carrier for Canada Post rather than accepting a promotion that he had been offered at work. This new position paid about the same but allowed him more freedom to set his hours. This allowed Dad to remain engaged in his number-one occupation: being a father. Years later Mom and Dad achieved financial freedom by living smartly, within their means, and by having an uncanny sixth sense for real estate deals. Today, they live debt-free on "Summer Hill Farms," a beautiful hundred-acre estate in the rolling hills north of Toronto. Not bad for a schoolteacher! But they would be the first to tell you that their real success in life was to raise fifteen children who deeply love and respect them. They dedicated their lives to teaching us the principles that would allow us to make the right choices in life so we could pass them on to our own families. Today, my parents are enjoying life in their golden years, surrounded by over sixty adoring grandchildren.

FIRST AT HOME

CARE must start at home with the ones closest to you. My parents believed that they had a lot to share, but that it starts with the children that they had been entrusted with. "If everyone sweeps in front of their own house, the streets will be clean," they would say. When the family business was formed, this same approach served as the basis for the development of the culture of CARE. Over the years this culture has positively impacted the lives of hundreds of team members and their families. Today as the same culture of CARE grows across the continent, that positive impact continues to increase exponentially. Who knows how many lives will be touched by what Mom and Dad started at home?

HUMBLE BEGINNINGS

It was a wonderful upbringing, and though we protested from time to time, my parents had the good sense to instill in us a strong work ethic. They told us that if you know how to and are willing to work hard, you could do well at whatever you do. All this work also kept us busy and out of trouble in our teen years. I can still feel the warm blankets being pulled off at 4:00 a.m. and my dad letting me know it was time to go to work. At fourteen years old I had a job on a dairy farm, where I was responsible for letting in the cows and feeding them before the milking team came in at 6:00 a.m. The farm was five miles from home, and I would ride my bike there before the sun came up. I can't honestly say I enjoyed those hard-labor jobs back then, but I sure was kept inspired by the responsibility I felt at that age. I worked at various farms, throwing hay bales and doing other chores during my summer holidays, right up until we started the business. As a young man my brother Tim was a natural at everything around the farm, including driving the big machinery. He spent his days plowing in the fields or cutting, baling, and raking hay while I, as the younger brother, was mostly assigned the task of mucking out stalls with a pitchfork.

Driving a tractor sounded more appealing to me, so I begged Farmer John to let me have a go at the tractor. One day he did; Farmer John had decided to take a chance on me and let me try my hand at something new.

It was a beautiful spring morning. The freshly cut hay needed to be raked so that it could dry on the bottom as well as the top before baling. The hay rake is a device that is attached to the back of a tractor. It has three wheels that rotate in succession. Each wheel has rake tines attached to it that lift the windrow of hay and flip it over as you drive the tractor forward. My job was to flip over all of the windrows of hay and then return to my regular duties. Farmer John pointed out that it was important not to drive too fast or too slow, and that the rake needed to be precisely at the right height in order to flip all of the hay without leaving any behind. Too low and you will break off the tines, too high and you will mess up the windrows and spread the hay all over the field. I remember Tim describing to me how he would get into "the zone" while operating a tractor for hours and how time would fly by while he tilled the land in perfectly straight lines.

As I began to rake the hay I had a huge smile on my face. Yes, I felt it, the smell of the hay the hum of the tractor. I was in "the zone." I envisioned myself operating a massive combine on the Canadian prairies, harvesting row after row of wheat. Everything was right in the world. I had found my vocation in life; I was going to be a farmer. In the corner of my eye I noticed Farmer John with a big smile on his face, waving at me. "Wow," I thought to myself, "I must be really doing a great job here!"

As I looked more closely however, I noticed he wasn't waving at me at all; he was motioning for me to stop, and the smile on his face was really an angry grimace. As I snapped out of "the zone," he handed me my well-worn pitchfork and asked me to get back to the barn. I said, "Do you want me to park the tractor?"

"No!" he barked, "Leave it right here."

It was then that I noticed that all of the tines on the hay rake had been broken off and that I had spent the last half hour spreading hay all over the field. I knew then and there that I wasn't going to grow up to be a farmer.

Somehow the gene for operating equipment had passed me by. As fate would have it, I would spend the next ten years like a square peg in a round hole, working in an equipment-intensive family business, trying hard to fit in, and trying not to damage anything. Tim, on the other hand, knew he liked working with machinery, with growing things, and being in the great outdoors. As it turned out, he would also develop his skills over the years as a savvy businessman.

ENTREPRENEURIAL BEGINNINGS

As high school came to an end, both Tim and I were pondering our careers. Tim investigated the possibility of following in our father's footsteps as a high school teacher, but he also loved the outdoors, had an entrepreneurial spirit, and was looking for a way to work together as a family. So he enrolled at Humber College in Toronto for the horticulture program, with the intention of starting a landscaping business. At the time a friend of my father, who had recently retired from a career as an arborist, gave me a tree-climbing harness and a set of climbing spurs. I had always climbed trees as a kid, and I think he gave them to me because he saw my potential. What I lacked in equipment expertise I certainly made up for in climbing ability and the lack of a fear of heights.

Tim took the horticulture program; I took the arboriculture major and became an arborist. Almost immediately we began to formulate our plans for launching our businesses. In 1989 I started Sunshine Tree and Shrub Care and Tim started Sunshine Landscape. We didn't have much money at the time to start our businesses, but Dad lent us an old trailer, a lawn mower, and a chainsaw. We hitched the trailer to our car, and off we went.

Though in separate businesses at the time, we would help each other out as needed. Tim was nineteen and I was eighteen. Our other brothers were still in school but helped out after class and during their summer holidays as required. As things progressed, each of our younger brothers found a place within the business. They joined not only because it seemed like a fun place to work but also because they saw a compelling business opportunity.

The landscape maintenance company began to really take off because of a customers-first mindset and a passion for quality service. Sunshine Tree Care was also doing well, but due to the technical nature of the business, I couldn't employ my younger brothers for much more than just cleanup and manual labor. The prospect of dragging branches all day provided little competition to the allure of driving lawn-mowing equipment, and soon all of my brothers and some of my sisters were working full time in the landscaping business. I was more or less working on my own.

My dad had begun working for Sunshine Landscape full time as well in an administrative and leadership role. He is a forward-thinking innovator, and with the intention of keeping our little company at the leading edge of the technology curve, he purchased a dial-up bid announcement system. With a 9600-baud modem, we would dial into a machine in Vancouver and download a list of potential projects that we could bid on. This concept so intrigued me that I began experimenting with computers, modems, and networking. When I stumbled upon the Internet a few years later, I asked Tim if I could roll my equipment and trucks into Sunshine Landscape and, with his help, start up an Internet service provider company. He agreed, and so I began a small ISP that served dial-up customers in our local dialing area. This didn't require much of my time, so I also worked at Sunshine Landscape in commercial sales and various other roles within the commercial maintenance division. We were still providing high-level tree trimming services at the time, and I clearly remember taking tech support calls from Internet customers while working in a tree, fifty feet off the ground, with a chainsaw strapped to my climbing belt.

As brothers we all have different personalities, passions, and skills, and I remember thinking I didn't have all of the skills needed to run a business successfully on my own. I am only really good at a few things. I could also see the power in the model that we as brothers were developing of "all for one, and one for all." Looking back, it seems that it was the diversity of skills amongst all of us that contributed to the success of the team. I use this lesson today when inviting people to my leadership team, and I make sure to surround myself with people whose different abilities make my weaknesses irrelevant and my strengths productive.

~

My passions are for things like art, branding, and marketing, and as such I would often spend a lot of time obsessing over colors, uniforms, designs, and logos. I am sure this was a source of frustration at times for Tim, who needed all hands on deck to get the work done. Being the practical guy that he is, Tim would say, "I'm glad that logo looks pretty, but we need to get out there and make some money. Jump in that truck and let's go." Rather than letting our differences become a source of unrest, we saw early on that with the right attitude, these differences could be leveraged for the good of the company.

My obsession with branding drove me to read anything I could find on the subject. I came across an article that spoke about the merits of white vehicles. The article used Federal Express (now FedEx) as an example of the right way to brand a fleet. At the time our trucks were whatever color they were when we bought them: two blue trucks, one green, and one red. I proposed that we design a "FedEx"-type fleet with white vehicles and nothing on them but our contact info and a big logo. We had a fairly complex logo at the time, with a tree, a sun, and the words "Sunshine Landscape." I went to work designing a green logo that simply said "Sunshine." As a test I had a white tarp installed over the back of one of our blue trucks and had the new logo installed. It looked great. The day after it was installed a customer said to me, "I see that truck everywhere!" I knew we were onto something.

We went ahead and painted all the trucks white and put on the new logos. Very quickly we became one of the most recognized brands in our area. It was the early '90s, and one of the big fashion trends of the day was a clothing and sunglasses brand called Vuarnet. Its t-shirt line was defined by bright colors with a large logo on the back. One day I saw someone walking down the street wearing a bright-yellow Vuarnet shirt, and I thought, "Wow, does that ever make a statement!" I went to a uniform company, ordered a yellow shirt, and had them iron press a big "Sunshine" logo on the back and a small one on the front. For a week I wore that shirt everywhere I went. That too received a lot of positive attention and great feedback from our customers. This soon became our uniform. We had begun establishing ourselves as a recognizable brand and, combined with exceptional work and genuine care, we were becoming a household name.

The Internet opportunity that I was building in the evenings and on weekends was a huge learning curve for me, and I poured myself into it. I learned all kinds of things about computers and networking and began to see how these technologies would completely change the way we conducted business in the future. Within a year or two our landscape business was growing again, and I had to make a decision about where to apply my new-found skills. I chose to sell the Internet business and to focus solely on using these technologies to help grow Sunshine Landscape. I took the networking skills I had learned and created a network in our office so that all calls could be recorded and sent to each of our workstations. When we returned to the office we synchronized our devices and could leave again with a full list of tasks. This was an era in which if you had a cell phone that fit in your pocket, people thought you were James Bond; it was a while before smartphones and mobile-Internet became the norm in our industry. We were one of the first companies in our landscape association to have a website, and years later we were early adapters of cloud technology, which helped catapult us into the franchising business. By embracing the mindset of "learn something new every day," many opportunities became available to us.

Marketing, to me, is about making promises. Whatever we say on our website and other marketing pieces, we know we have an obligation to deliver. Seeing a need for 24/7 live-dispatch during the snow season, I decided to advertise this as one of our offerings. At the time we couldn't afford to staff a call center 24/7, so I decided to take the job upon myself. That year just happened to be one of the busiest snow seasons in our history, and I was on the phone many nights talking to customers. Although exhausted, I enjoyed the chance to get to know our customers better and to help them find solutions to their needs. Because we were getting hit by back-to-back storms, I forwarded our hotline to my cell phone, jumped into a plow truck, and helped out with the plowing.

On one occasion, I had just finished plowing a commercial property and was heading to the next when I got a call on the hotline. "Peter, I don't know what kind of people you have working for you, but I'm not happy. Your guy just plowed our place and left and I don't think he did a very good job."

"I'm sorry," I said. "I'll send him right back. I will find out what went wrong and deal with it. Perhaps some training might be in order!" After I hung up, I got the guilty plow operator right back there—by turning my vehicle around and going back to the property of the customer who had just called me. I re-plowed his place properly this time.

The next few years provided more growth and development. We continued to build our company and brand on quality workmanship and genuine care. We started to attract larger commercial clients and had grown our capacity to be able to take care of the needs of one of North America's largest auto manufacturing plants without turning our backs on our earliest residential clients. Some of our first residential maintenance customers, who took a chance on a couple of kids with a lawnmower, are still customers of ours more than twenty years later.

Each of us put our bodies, hearts, and minds into the tasks at hand with drive and ambition. We worked long hours and often right through weekends and holidays. We also played hard and had a lot of fun. We bought a motor boat together, and if we could finish all of our work by noon on a Saturday, we would all head up to Cook's Bay and spend the afternoon waterskiing and wakeboarding until we were too tired to go on. We didn't own our own lake house at the time, but we added that to our dream list for the future. One of our principles is "have fun and love what you do," and we were having fun.

Position and title mean very little in a family business like ours. If you tried to pull rank on your brother, he'd tell you to go fly a kite. We never had titles back then, and amongst ourselves we still don't. But when asked we were happy to reply, "Brother number four," "Brother number five," and so on. When I was registering Tim and myself for a conference, the registrar said that we needed a title for the name card. I told her, "Tim's title is HBIC."

"What does that stand for?" she asked.

"That is 'Head Brother In Charge,'" I replied. Being in business with nine brothers taught each of us that, no matter your title, you are not a leader if no one wants to follow you. And no one will follow you if you haven't earned their permission to be led. You can't fake leadership; there are no shortcuts. Tim, as the founder of Sunshine Landscape and the eldest brother, naturally held a leadership position, but we only followed his lead because he had earned our trust and admiration.

Despite the hard work and very little free time, we remained driven and inspired by our clear and compelling dreams and goals. One habit we formed early on as brothers was the ability to paint a clear picture of what the future would look like if we continued to work hard. It was during these years that I learned about the power of goal setting. Some of my brothers seemed to have found their passion, and I could tell that they loved what they did. It was evident by the success they were having in their roles. I, on the other hand, although working hard, felt like something was missing. I wasn't passionate about my job yet. I felt as though I were still searching for my calling.

One day a business opportunity in advertising was presented to Tim. Although unrelated to our existing business, it seemed to have merit. The landscaping business was running smoothly, so Tim asked me if I would explore the concept as a possible diversification to our family business. I eagerly accepted the challenge, thinking maybe I would find the missing piece to my happiness. Although I didn't know it at the time, I would indirectly stumble upon what would later become my passion.

My brother Seth joined me in this endeavor, and for the next year or so we began to learn the advertising business. We ran a test pilot in Toronto and in Los Angeles. During this time I found myself in situations where I had to pitch the concept to both potential clients and potential business partners. In one of those meeting with a hotel executive in Niagara Falls, I was introduced to the concept of franchising. Up until that meeting I had never really investigated the franchising model, and so I began reading everything I could find about the concept.

I came across the book *Profitable Partnerships* by Greg Nathan, where he describes the power of franchising as a model for growth, strengthened through the sharing of best practices and knowledge. As I continued reading, Nathan explained the business model as a unique relationship where independent business owners work together for the good of the whole brand. I found it intriguing and also very similar to the structure of our "all for one and one for all" family business. Although the advertising opportunity I was researching did not prove to be a viable concept for the North American market, I did learn valuable information about franchising that would change the course of our business forever.

A few years later we were at my parents' house for our year-end planning and strategy meeting. Several of us were married at this point and had children. Our family situations were changing and so were our priorities. There was much discussion around our need and desire to spend more time with our young families while balancing the need for the continued growth of our business.

That's when I had an epiphany moment! It was like a lightbulb going off in my mind, and I blurted out, "We could franchise!"

"What?" came the collective outcry.

"Yes, we could franchise our business model and open locations that will service clients the Sunshine way, across the country!" After a few initial reality checks and the odd objection, we all agreed that this could work for us.

This was a huge step. Franchising is a completely different business model than what we were used to. We were experts in the landscape management business but completely new to the world of franchising. I believe the franchise business is all about training, coaching, writing, and speaking as well as developing and documenting systems in manuals and training programs. These are not the skills typically required to be successful in the landscape management business. This type of work, however, was right up my alley. I was given the go-ahead to lead this new initiative.

It felt as if everything I had ever done to date had prepared me for this day. I was ready to do this job and to OWN IT! My experiences in the Internet business and marketing concepts had forced me to develop skills that were very useful in my new role within the company. I once read that when something you are good at lines up with something that you love to do, you have a good hobby. When what you are good at lines up with what you love doing and that is something that the market needs—you have found your calling. This is how it was for me.

For the next two years I poured my heart, mind, and soul into the tasks at hand. We documented everything we ever knew about the right and wrong ways to operate a landscape management business in operations manuals. We developed software to handle multiple locations, and we drew up disclosure documents and franchise agreements.

FINDING MY VOICE

A year or so later I was appointed CEO of the company. Something amazing happened the moment I received that appointment, and it has a very important lesson in it. I learned the power of believing and trusting in people, even when they may not yet believe in themselves. When I was entrusted with the position I instantly felt a great weight of responsibility. I felt like the captain of the ship, responsible for the problems and also for the solutions.

My new position highlighted my weaknesses, but I was inspired to begin studying, reading, and learning everything I could to fill in the gaps. I attended every conference I could that applied to my field, and I worked through most of my weekends and holidays. I enrolled in the ICFE program offered by the International Franchise Association and ultimately graduated as a Certified Franchise Executive. I needed little outside motivation or prompting. The new title didn't come with a corner office, an executive assistant, or a huge pay raise, and yet I felt a powerful inner drive and ambition to excel in my new role. What was it that gave me the energy and drive to work around the clock and dedicate so much passion to my job? Where was my inspiration coming from? Discovering the source of this inspiration became important to me. If I could identify the source, then I could offer similar conditions for my team and help them find their passion. Imagine the mountains that can be moved when the whole team is working with unbridled passion rather than just putting in hours!

The most common belief in business seems to be that money alone motivates, but for me it was more than that. Here are the four points that I discovered as the source of my inspiration:

- I was motivated by a salary that was fair and sufficient. I also didn't have to worry about being paid. I could see the potential in a business that gave me the opportunity to work harder and earn more money.

- I was inspired by the autonomy that came with my new role. I had the freedom to take ownership of my job, set my own priorities, goals, and vision, recruit my own team, and build a unique culture.

- I was inspired by the opportunity to work at something I enjoy and the chance to grow and become a master at it.

- Lastly, I was inspired to be a part of an organization that not only makes a profit, but also can do good. Building a company that helps others achieve their dreams is very rewarding and gave me a real sense of purpose and significance.

These are the same reasons many people want to be an entrepreneur or get into business in the first place. Why wouldn't we create these same conditions for our team? We want to attract and retain entrepreneurial types, not people who are just looking to put in eight hours and go home. Offer anything less than the conditions described above, and the right kind of people will go looking for a more challenging and fulfilling vocation elsewhere.

A LESSON LEARNED

Experience is a great teacher. One of the ways we learn as a company is from our mistakes, and over the years we've made plenty of them. By 2007 we were adding new locations and expanding rapidly. On the surface things looked good; the numbers were solid. However, in addition to collecting financial data, we were watching other indicators, and there was trouble on the horizon. The most important people in our business, our customers, were not happy. After eighteen years of nearly impeccable service, our customer loyalty scores were starting to trend downward. Some of our most loyal customers were beginning to communicate to us that the level of care that they had become accustomed to and that had attracted them to our brand was starting to decline. For a "Customers First" company like ours, even a slight drop in the level of happiness our customers were experiencing was unacceptable and alarming.

We knew that we needed to quickly address the situation. Creating a remarkable experience for our customers was what our brand was known for, and we were not going to stand by and let that change. We had been taught from childhood to look inward when we see a problem. So that's exactly what we did. We asked ourselves: What are we doing or not doing that might be contributing to this problem? After listening to our customers and our franchise partners, we decided that a lack of training might be to blame.

Around this time, I attended a seminar by Jim Paluch,[4] a green industry consultant, who spoke about lean management and process improvement. I also stumbled across the book *The E-myth Revisited* by Michael Gerber,[5] and I became overwhelmed with the realization that we needed to do a better job of documenting our systems. From Gerber I learned about the importance of documenting systems and processes, and from Paluch I learned to be "hard on the system and soft on the people." Perhaps with better operations manuals and a completely revamped training program we could improve this situation.

Thus began the creation of an updated set of operations manuals and user guides that would document and explain every detail of how to run a successful franchise location. To help with this massive undertaking, we engaged a franchise consultant by the name of Perry Maisonneuve.[6] He had worked with many companies in the Canadian Franchise Association and came highly recommended. One of Perry's skills was to look at each system from the perspective of a new franchisee and ask questions that required us to distill our knowledge in a way that could be easily consumed. When finally completed, we had a fully documented system containing 473 pages of information.

---

4   Jim's mission is to energize a trillion people. See more at www.jphorizons.com.

5   Emyth International: www.emyth.com

6   Northern Lights Franchise Consultants: www.franchiseservices.ca

THE THREE-LEGGED STOOL

We call this system our "three-legged stool of success." The entire system consists of a Business Management, Technical Services, and Customer CARE manual, each component comprising a leg of the stool. Each of the three sections has three chapters, creating a three-legged stool for each business focus area. Each focus area has distinct systems that create efficiency for the business owner and a remarkable experience for the customer.

The three-legged stool concept helps us to illustrate the importance of developing competence in each of these distinct areas. Take one leg away and the stool becomes shaky. Take two legs away and you won't be sitting on the stool of success for very long. Many small businesses operate on shaky ground for this very reason.

In the Customer CARE manual, the three sections are:

1. **Marketing**—how to get the phone to ring;

2. **Sales**—how to prepare an accurate, professional and profitable quotation;

3. **CARE**—how to "wow" customers with service and earn their loyalty for life!

In the Technical Services manual, we documented all of our operations systems into three categories:

1. **Ongoing Operations**—what we do on a daily, weekly, and monthly basis to maintain smooth and safe operations;

2. **Summer Operations**—summer-specific systems that produce world-class service and create operational efficiency;

3. **Winter Operations**—winter-specific systems that produce the same outcomes during the winter season.

The Business Management manual contains our accounting, planning, and people systems.

1. **Planning**—how to budget and plan for sustainable growth;

2. **Accounting**—how to make sure you hit your financial targets;

3. **People**—how to find, recruit, and retain a world-class team.

The end result of our efforts enables a new franchise partner with relatively little experience to read our "playbook," understand and implement the systems, and be successful. This was our road map to success! These systems helped us excel in the past, and we were certain that anyone who learned and implemented them would share the same results . . . or so we thought. From the contents of the manual we developed training programs, thirty-two modules in all, and we began conducting three-to-five–day classes to retrain everyone in the system.

I was excited to start the new year. Each of our franchise locations had a copy of the manual, and everyone had been trained on it. We learned later that it would have been better to start with the "why": the reasons behind the systems and the principles on which they were designed. We had started with the "what" and the "how," and as a result the operations manual was initially received by some franchisees as a heavy book of restrictive rules. We should have known better; we weren't raised that way. We weren't handed a book of rules and told to "comply or else." We were taught the principles and values first. If the "why" isn't understood, the rules are mostly unenforceable.

> "When mores are sufficient, laws are unnecessary; when mores are insufficient, laws are unenforceable."
>
> —Émile Durkheim, nineteenth-century sociologist

Prior to the release of the updated operations manual we had been trying to support and teach our business systems by traveling around to each location, doing on-site training and coaching. This was a drain on our resources, and despite our efforts, our famous customer experience continued to suffer. We seemed unable to get the message out fast enough. We knew that we couldn't expand our franchise network until we solved this problem.

At that time our solution was to send one of "the brothers" in to fix things up if there was a problem. For a time this management technique was very effective. Each of my nine brothers had grown up in the business and were strong on the technical and operational procedures. They knew how to work and they cared deeply about the business. They had grown up in a culture where we put the needs of our customers first. Situations that arose with customers, team members, or vendors were solved within minutes when one of the brothers showed up. This was not just a job for them; it was their business—their brand. I recall something that our consultant Perry said at the time: "Peter, at some point you are going to run out of brothers. If your only method for gaining compliance and brand alignment is to send one of you out, you will eventually run out of brothers." He was right!

OVERCOMING BARRIERS TO GROWTH

In his book *The 21 Irrefutable Laws of Leadership*, John C. Maxwell talks about the law of the lid. This is where an entrepreneur or business owner hits his limitations and becomes the "lid" of the organization. He is unable or unwilling to build up other leaders and relinquish control to them, thus limiting the organization's ability to grow beyond his immediate reach. The rugged individuality and command-and-control management style of the boss, which had served him well up to this point, has now become his barrier to growth.

In many family businesses that are infused with trust, family members work in such a way that enables growth well beyond the reach of the founder or manager. However, the law of the lid can catch up and take effect. The family comes to the extent of its reach, and growth stagnates. My brothers and I knew that if we were to avoid becoming the lid of our own organization, we would need to empower new leaders in the company who would think and act as we did. We would need to invite leaders to our team who were as driven and inspired as we were.

We had experienced this before. In the early days we had several lawn maintenance teams comprised of two or three brothers per team. But as our business grew it became necessary for us to add more teams. So we invited our first "non-brother" into the company. This was a new concept and if it felt strange for us; I can only imagine what it must have been like for him! Expansion continued, and eventually we had one brother per three-person team, in the role of team leader. Ten teams was our new lid. How could we grow beyond that? We had no more brothers! Eventually we had to entrust a nonfamily member as a team leader. CARE Leadership concepts like proper delegation and developing a principled and productive team helped us overcome these barriers to growth. Before we began franchising we had over twenty-five teams in operation and employed over seventy team members, with each brother managing a portion of the operations. This was our business in 2005.

As we grew our franchise system to a new level, the release of the updated operations manual and the new training and support program was going to be our first step towards overcoming the new barrier to growth we were facing. This was a new challenge for us. Building self-motivated, self-governing leaders who would uphold our brand from multiple, geographically separated locations proved more challenging than accomplishing the same outcome from one central location. The inability to interact face-to-face on a daily basis was a new complexity, and we had to find a solution.

Over the next few years, the manuals and the increased focus on training really helped us get the message out to our franchise partners, and thankfully we noticed a turnaround. Our customer loyalty scores began to steadily climb back up to where they were prior to franchising. This was a great success, and for a while the pressure eased up on the support team.

SOLVING THE MULTILOCATION CHALLENGE

We realized that we needed a system for quantifying brand and system alignment across our network. So we developed a system called TAGS™, which stands for Team and Truck, Admin and Accounting, GC3™/CLEAR™ (our quality control protocols), and Shop and Operations. The TAGS system is a more than 200-point checklist that helps franchisees rate themselves on system implementation. It highlights areas of success and opportunities for improvement. Our Franchise

Coaches use the TAGS system as a coaching tool and to help monitor and benchmark the progress of each of our locations.

When we started tracking brand alignment using the TAGS system and measured the results, we started noticing irregularities. Everyone was trained on the same materials, everyone had the same manual, and everyone had similar competency, yet the results were different. That's when we realized that there was a missing piece to the puzzle: character.

We seemed to have some franchisees that "cared" more than others. The ones that cared were working hard to implement systems and take care of their people and their customers. Although each were at different levels of understanding and implementation, at least they were on the path. You could see and feel the enthusiasm and excitement as they learned how to be better at their business.

However, the ones that didn't care as much required all kinds of extra attention, policing, and watching over. They needed to be followed up on, monitored, and reminded. Their lack of care manifested itself in poor profitability, poor quality, and poor customer retention. We had the systems, the training programs, the ongoing support, and the operations manuals, but we had not yet successfully infused the culture that was necessary to implement those systems. We realized that to entrust someone with our brand and our customers, we needed people with the skills to do the job properly and the character to do it with integrity.

Teaching someone the technical or hard skills to run one of our businesses was relatively easy, especially now that we had systematized every aspect of the operation and perfected the training methods. By doing this we had removed much of the complexity and confusion that most small businesses face. Teaching someone to care, however, is different. Care is seen as a soft skill, not the type of thing landscapers often get together and talk about. You are more likely to hear more macho conversations about trucks and equipment or the guy they just fired.

CARE is a whole new way of thinking, a whole new paradigm. If someone is stuck in the "boss" mindset, it is almost futile to try to integrate these new systems into their operations. It won't work. It would be analogous to installing the latest piece of computer software on an outdated operating system. If it worked at all, it would be slow and prone to errors. With the wrong operating system, you can't derive the full benefit from that wonderful new piece of software. In the same way, someone in the "boss" mindset will never be able to successfully install new systems based on CARE Leadership unless they first understand and internalize the principles on which those systems are based.

In 2009 I did an interview for an article in *FranchiseCanada Magazine* about our franchise system. A copy of that article made it into the hands of Mike Bidwell, president and COO of one of the world's largest service-based franchise systems, The Dwyer Group, in Waco, Texas. He was intrigued by our story and passed it on to Dwyer's CEO, Dina Dwyer-Owens, who called to introduce herself. We had a great conversation and found out that we had very similar backgrounds. I hadn't heard of The Dwyer Group before, so after the call I jumped online and began researching the company. I immediately recognized their well-respected brands: Mr. Rooter®, The Glass Dr.®, Mr. Electric®, Mr. Appliance®, Aire Serve®, and Rainbow International®. The dominant message that came up in my initial searches was The Dwyer Group Code of Values™. "Here is a company that really puts a lot of stock in values," I thought to myself. "Either this is great PR, or they really do care."

Up to this point we had always lived by an unwritten code. We believed that values are caught more readily than taught, and we built our great company culture by showing through example what we valued. This worked well for us at a single-location setting where we could interact with team members on a regular basis. But now our brand was represented in twenty-four different locations with twenty-four different personalities leading each location. We were in danger of losing the culture we had worked so hard to build. While leading by example is still the first step in culture building, we needed a new way to get our message out there. One day I received a package in the mail from Dina. She had sent me a few copies of her book *Live RICH*. In the book she described how to build success in your company and your life with a proven code of values. I couldn't put the book down. Dina and The Dwyer Group had gone through a situation similar to ours, and it struck a chord with me.

Thus began the journey of articulating our own values. We had to put in writing the code that we had lived by all these years: an unwritten code passed down to us by our parents that had helped us build a great culture and brand. For this we would have to go back to our early days in the business. What were the reasons that made us all care about our customers and our business so much? How did we infuse this care into our culture? How do we define care? What are the values and principles that make up a culture of care, and how do we make sure that this culture continues to define us as we expand and grow? We realized how important the culture of care had been to our success and how it would be vital to our success going forward.

There is no quick fix when it comes to The Culture of CARE. It must be deliberately nurtured and developed. Systems can be duplicated and copied, but a culture cannot. It is in our DNA and is something that cannot be taken by a competitor.

~

The word "Care" had always been in our vernacular and used throughout our marketing materials. Care was infused in our corporate identity, and as we identified the values that meant the most to us we
lined them up to form the acronym C.A.R.E., which stands for: Customers first, Attitude, Respect, and Enjoy life in the process. I remember thinking that it's one thing to say that we care, but how do we
show that we care? The answer became our values statement that we
call The Code of CARE.

> **THE CODE OF CARE™**
>
> We show that we **CARE** by putting the needs of our
> **C**ustomers first, by always having a positive and helpful
> **A**ttitude, and by treating everyone and everything with
> **R**espect. By living our code of values we
> **E**njoy life in the process.

This values statement could now be easily memorized by every
one who worked for our brands, both at the head office and at each
franchise location.

To make sure that these all-important values remain top-of-
mind, we incorporated them into our daily huddle, a quick, seven-
to-ten-minute, high-energy, stand-up focus meeting conducted first
thing every day. It starts with a recital of the Code of CARE and ends
with a loud, energetic cheer. The huddle is one of our most important culture drivers and allows us all to reconnect with our core values
every day before taking care of our customers.

When we first introduced the Code of CARE, those who didn't really care became uncomfortable with the new emphasis on values and principles. Some of them left on their own; some had to be counseled out. We knew one thing: we would not be successful at becoming a company admired for its culture of CARE if we had people on the team who didn't believe in it. Because it is easier to train someone on the skill side of a job than it is to teach them respect or a good attitude, we decided to spend our energy on inviting to the team only those people who were predisposed to these values. We became more selective on who we invited to our team, both at the home office and as franchise partners. We redesigned our recruitment process to focus on both values and technical competency, but with an emphasis on values. We redesigned our questionnaire process to help us get a better feel for the candidate's predisposition to our values and their understanding and application of them. We call it "The Culture of CARE Questionnaire™."

We redesigned our team member evaluation and review process to include our core values and principles so that we could encourage and reinforce the right behaviors. We call this procedure the "People Builder Process™." We realized that if we wanted our values to be more than just words on our lobby wall, we needed to hire and fire based on them. In fact, our goal is to infuse our values into everything we do, including our systems, processes, words, and actions.

Very quickly we saw a change take place, first at the home office, then among our franchise partners, and finally in our front-line team members. The culture of CARE was taking hold across the entire network. The need for compliance monitoring dropped. Interest in training and professional development increased. Team member turnover decreased, and customer loyalty increased to its highest levels since we began franchising.

EXPANSION INTO THE USA

In February 2009 I flew to San Diego to attend the International Franchise Association conference and to meet Dina Dwyer-Owens, who was the Chairwoman of the IFA at the time. She had set up a meeting with me to discuss ways we might be able to work together. It was a good meeting, and we both agreed to keep talking. A few months later Tim and I went to Texas to meet The Dwyer Group executive team. They explained that they were interested in buying our company. We weren't interested in selling, but we agreed that we should find a way to work together in some capacity. We were impressed with their team and could see that their values went much deeper than words.

Over the next six months we met with Dina, and Mike Bidwell, president of The Dwyer Group, and spent a lot of time on the phone discussing particulars. Tim and I were repeatedly impressed by the open and honest way in which they conducted business. Here were two executives of an 800 million–dollar company who truly walked their talk.

I recall in one round of negotiations Mike Bidwell pointed out a clause that we had proposed in the letter of intent that he felt would not be a win-win situation. He said, "I'd take a look at that clause. I don't think the way it's worded would be in your best interest." We read it from a new perspective, saw the potential oversight, and thanked him for pointing it out; we hadn't seen it that way. They always had the best interest of both parties in mind and stayed true to their values.

WHAT'S IN A NAME?

Sunshine Brands and The Dwyer Group were close to making a deal, but we had one major hurdle left to cross. In October 2009, Dina,

Mike, and Robert Tunmire, executive VP of The Dwyer Group, were on a due diligence visit to our National Training Center in Orangeville. We met over dinner, where they broke some unpleasant news. "We love your system and want to do a deal with you, but we can't do it under the name 'Sunshine,'" Dina said.

I felt as if I had been punched in the stomach. Our operating brand at the time was Sunshine Grounds Care, but because "Sunshine" is such a common word, it had been used and trademarked numerous times under various other applications. This was especially true in places like the "Sunshine State" of Florida, where there seemed to be a Sunshine Landscape company in every county. According to The Dwyer Group's attorneys, we would need to come up with another name before we could move ahead. My mom had come up with the name "Sunshine" from our last name, van Stralen, which can be loosely translated from the Dutch language to "from the sun's rays," or "Sunshine." We had spent eighteen years building a reputation around the name, and here we were being asked to change it.

The truth is that a few years earlier, as we made our first forays into the States, our trademark lawyers in Washington had advised me to start looking for a new name or be ready to defend our right to use it. The thought of changing our identity was so distasteful to me that I didn't even mention it to anyone. Having little experience in trademark law at the time, I simply suggested that we would deal with it when it became necessary. The Dwyer Group, on the other hand, had all kinds of experience in this area, and they had decided it would be too costly to defend. It had become a reality: if we wanted to expand into the US, we were going to have to change our name!

What would happen with our existing customers and our franchise partners in Canada? Would we lose our identity and our brand equity? Would customers leave us, or would it be as Shakespeare expressed: would a rose by any other name smell as sweet?

We were again at a big bend in the road. Someone once told me, "A bend in the road is not the end of the road, unless you fail to make the turn." But we were so attached to our name and the rich history behind it that this was almost the end of the road for us. Luckily we also saw a compelling opportunity and kept an open mind.

It was time for us to consider what a brand really is. Is it a logo, name, design, shape, and color that our customers are loyal to, or is it something more than that? No, a logo is just a graphical representation of our company's identity. A brand, on the other hand, is created by the culture of the company and the resulting experiences, stories, and memories that people have collected over the years. Surely our customers would understand. Their loyalty, we reasoned, was to us, our systems, and to our people—not our name. No matter what name we ended up with, we were convinced that our customers would remain loyal if we remained loyal to them. So we agreed to start looking for a new name.

The Dwyer Group creative team got together to brainstorm names; my brothers and I did the same. Finding a name for local use is one thing, but finding a name that can be used internationally is a whole different matter. First of all it has to appeal to the right demographic, convey the right message, and most importantly, not be already in use. With the hundreds of thousands of companies out there, that was a very tall order.

Over the next several days we sat as a team and came up with dozens of names. Some were funny, some ridiculous, and some were pretty good. However, all of the ones we liked were already widely in use or previously trademarked. Eventually the team had to get about their regular business duties, and so I retreated to my office to continue brainstorming. My love of branding and marketing kicked in, and soon I found myself in "the zone."—but this time I wasn't breaking the tines off a hay rake! Maybe I should elaborate a little.

Some people call it "flow" or "the flow phenomenon." I looked it up on Wikipedia, which states, "Flow is the mental state of operation in which a person performing an activity is fully immersed in a feeling of energized focus, full involvement, and enjoyment in the process of the activity. In essence, flow is characterized by complete absorption in what one does."[7] All of my experiences in business and in life had prepared me for this major hurdle we were facing. My love of what I was doing and the compelling opportunity ahead of me allowed me to get into a state of flow. I've experienced flow while riding my bike up a large hill, where I've reached the top and it seemed effortless, or at various other times while working.

On this particular day I began typing all of the words and phrases that meant anything to us. I typed "Grounds Care," because that was our core service and was also in our name: "Sunshine Grounds Care." People had always called us "the Sunshine Boys" and sometimes "the Sunshine Guys," so I typed those words as well. I typed in CARE, because I felt that that was our real identity. I started matching up and grouping the words that seemed to fit together, and then I saw it: "The Grounds Guys." That was it! I knew immediately that the name suited us.

I quickly searched for the domain online, and to my surprise it was available. I immediately registered GroundsGuys.com, .ca, .au, and .eu, as well as every variation I could find. I called my trademark lawyer and had him file an application for registration in Canada. Then I quickly did up a rough logo design using our existing colors, gold and green, and added a leaf from one of our other marketing

---

7   Source: *Wikipedia* (http://en.wikipedia.org/wiki/Flow_(psychology)).

pieces. I pasted the logo onto a photo of a team member and also on a truck and trailer and emailed them to Dina. She liked it right away and immediately filed for registration in the US. Together we hired a branding company out of New York City to do a thorough market study on the name. They conducted focus groups all over America and it was widely accepted.

We have a lot of women working in our company, and I wanted their opinion as to whether the word "guys" in our name would be interpreted as too masculine. To test my theory I found a group of men and women talking in our lunchroom one day and I said, "Hey guys, can you come here for a minute?" They all responded to the call, so I said, "Thanks, you just answered my question." "Guys" seems to be a common, casual term used to address both males and females.

The name was officially adopted and we were able to move ahead with the deal between Sunshine Brands and The Dwyer Group to build The Grounds Guys® brand in the USA. In Canada we began the rebranding process immediately and today we operate as The Grounds Guys® at all of our locations. Our customers didn't leave us, proving to us that their loyalty was based on the way we treated them rather than the name we operated under. For a few months we co-branded and then fully transitioned over to our new name. The brand equity that we had built over many years was transferred to the new name as well.

I have the opportunity to speak with many entrepreneurs and families who are struggling with the decision to make a name change in order to realize a compelling opportunity. When I speak to them now, I do so with empathy and a much clearer understanding of what they are going through. To this day we enjoy an open and sharing relationship with The Dwyer Group, where both parties lookout for the wellbeing of the other. The brand continues to grow well beyond our expectations.

OUR STORY CONTINUES ...

Today, my brothers and I still work together in a spirit of unity and cooperation. The structure of our family business has grown to the point where each of us operates separate businesses in strategic partnership. Each brother is passionate about his own specialty and pursuing his business opportunity. We regularly meet to seek each other's council. As for me, I have found my vocation at Sunshine Brands. Our mission is to share the Culture of CARE, and that is what my team and I are passionate about.

THE RESULT = A CULTURE-DRIVEN COMPANY

My story, although not unique, has led me to where we are today. Upon reflection, here are a few of the benefits that we derive from a company driven by the Culture of CARE:

1. Team Members who look for ways to go above and beyond to create a remarkable experience for customers and colleagues;
2. a fun work environment, where people love what they do;
3. enthusiastic Team Members who take ownership of their work, hold themselves accountable, and achieve maximum results;
4. a culture of continuous improvement in systems and professional development;
5. an environment where leadership is a choice, not a position;
6. an informed and engaged team driven by open and respectful communication;

7. a trusting culture that removes barriers to optimal performance;

8. a strong sense of significance, purpose, and fulfillment.

This allows us to enjoy life, achieve exceptional results, and reach our goals while becoming better people in the process. Not a bad way to spend the day!

HOW TO BUILD A CULTURE OF CARE IN YOUR ORGANIZATION

Now that you've read our story, you may have realized that you have similar goals or dreams for your company. The good news is that you can achieve similar results in your organization, bringing about a complete transformation of the culture. You don't have to wait until you have a position of leadership or management, because leadership is a choice, not a position. CARE Leadership is contagious and can have a positive effect on everyone around you. In this chapter I will share with you all of the secrets I have learned over the years about how to build a Culture of CARE within an organization. We will discuss how to make sure that your values become the standard by which your entire team operates, rather than just meaningless words that only a few buy into.

START WITH THE PRINCIPLES

Principles are timeless, universal, natural laws that operate around us whether we believe in them or not. They are not practices, policies, or systems; principles are the "why" behind them. While the systems we follow govern and guide our actions, principles govern the outcome of those actions.

To illustrate the difference between principles and practices I often use the following example: Let's say a parent wanted to teach her child about the dangers of climbing trees. She begins training him in safe climbing techniques, and over time the mother can successfully teach her child to be a safe tree climber. But one day, they are visiting a friend in the city, and she notices her child playing on a high ledge, way above the street. She calls up to him, "Get off that ledge! It's dangerous; you could fall!" The problem is that all of his training to date has been around the practice of safe tree climbing. He is unfamiliar with this new situation and the dangers of high ledges. His training has been practice-based, and because of a lack of understanding of the underlying principle (the dangers of ignoring gravity), he is unable to adapt. The parent has to watch over her child constantly and is afraid to let him out of her sight. By contrast, if this parent had focused on teaching an understanding of gravity, the child would be able to apply what he knew about gravity to all high places, not just trees. When his friends dare him to climb up onto the roof, his understanding of the principle of gravity will guide him to make a wise decision. Once he has demonstrated a full understanding of the principle and his actions and practices are in alignment, trust is developed. The parent can now relax and take comfort in the fact that her child's decisions will be based on an understanding of principles, not just practices.

We believe it is best to apologize quickly when we make a mistake or let down a customer, but we do not make this a hard-and-fast policy. If we did, we would have people apologizing in situations where it might not be appropriate, and we would also run the risk of having people apologize verbally but not mean it at all. Our customers would pick up on this. Instead, we recruit people who are guided by the principle "Be Humble." Based on this underlying principle, we can rely on our team members to offer sincere apologies in the appropriate situations.

Another reason to start with the principles is that they bring stability amidst constant change. Software changes, equipment changes, laws come and go, procedures and practices change . . . but principles remain constant. The need to adapt our operating procedures and practices was never more evident than when our company began to expand into other countries, states, and provinces, each with different laws, climates, and cultures. Leadership based on sound principles will give your team a solid foundation to stand on and will allow you to embrace change, adapt quickly to it, and thrive in the midst of it.

KNOW THE DIFFERENCE BETWEEN BRAND COMPLIANCE AND BRAND ALIGNMENT

We use a task management system that is populated with reminders designed to help franchise owners with time-management and productivity. One of our brand systems is to update tasks as they are completed and to prioritize your list daily. A long list of overdue and incomplete tasks indicates that someone is not using, and therefore not deriving benefit from, the system. From experience we know this will cause problems down the road, so our Franchise Coaches (FCs) will monitor it as a key performance indicator. I recall a conversation with one franchisee who was constantly showing "overdue" tasks on his list and became tired of the constant reminders to update it. One day he joyfully proclaimed that he had found a solution. His wife would now log in and update his list for him. With a daily updated list, he had achieved compliance. The problem was that he was still receiving no benefit from the system. Brand alignment wasn't achieved until he saw the benefit in the task management system and formed the daily habit of using it *himself*.

WE BECOME THE WORDS WE USE

Someone once told me "we become the words we use," and it stuck with me. To build a strong and unique culture, it is important to carefully select your words. Words are powerful. They can build up or tear down, inspire or demotivate. Used repeatedly over time, the words we use begin to shape our behaviors and actions. In our industry, the word "crew" is commonly used, but we prefer the word "team." There is nothing wrong with the word "crew," but we think that belonging to a "team" helps keep the idea of teamwork and cooperation top-of-mind. We use the terms "team member" and "team leader" instead of "employee." Again, there is nothing wrong with the word "employee," but "team member" fits our culture better and helps to reinforce the value of teamwork.

THINK LONG TERM AND THINK BIG!

Shortsighted thinking can be detrimental to CARE Leadership and the Culture of CARE. CARE Leadership is about building other care leaders on your team at all levels of the organization. This takes time. Building a strong culture requires leaders to look past the current situation and focus on what can be, versus what is. The principles and practices discussed in this book aren't quick fixes or silver bullets. In fact, quick fixes usually break down just as quickly. Real, quantifiable results, however, will take place as you integrate CARE Leadership principles into your organization.

In some organizations, long-term investments in people, like training and leadership development, often take a back seat, because short-term thinking sees those activities as a drain on the bank account. If thinking is shortsighted, why would one invest in education or mastery programs that might take years to complete and even longer to produce results? Why invest in long-term relationships with customers that will pay off way down the road? People with short-term thinking are likely to look for the highest and most immediate pay back, even if it causes them problems later. "He's toxic and is doing damage to our brand; we need to do something about it," a team member says to her manager. "Let's just leave things as they are," says the shortsighted manager. "He's a big earner."

When designing systems for our franchise network, even though we were operating in only one city, we always asked ourselves the question, "Will this system work nationally?" Start acting today like the company you want to become in the future, otherwise you will never get there.

Why would a short-term thinker give to charity or to the community? "I'll give back when I'm rich," they say, like the robber barons of old who spent their lifetimes exploiting people and natural resources for their own selfish gain while amassing huge fortunes. Then, in their twilight years, out of guilt and a fear of the afterlife, they gave away most of their fortunes in hopes of redemption.

> Start acting today like the company you want to become in the future, otherwise you will never get there.

Working hard to build wealth for yourself and your family is what our free society and free economy is all about. But it is important to realize that only wealth combined with happiness brings true success, and that this happiness comes from serving others.

PROMOTE FOR THE RIGHT REASONS

When I was in my mid-twenties I had a discussion with a team member about his future career. He was a recent immigrant from Poland and started with us as a general laborer. He was in his late forties and was a father with two children. I told him he could be a manager someday and was encouraging him to look into what it would take to upgrade his skills. A little frustrated, he replied in his broken English, "Luke is boss before I'm boss." Luke is our youngest brother and was only about fourteen at the time. I could tell that he saw this as a dead-end job, because he thought that the seemingly endless line of brothers would always be promoted first, due to their last name. This is a very common mistake made in family businesses, and it makes it hard to attract good people to the team. Our philosophy is that the best person for the job is promoted.

DON'T LOOK FOR SHORTCUTS

In light of all the news around the use of performance-enhancing drugs in sports, I have been thinking about the natural human weakness that tempts us to try and take shortcuts to greatness. Trying to bypass natural laws and principles may work for a time, but this will eventually catch up with you.

Leadership cannot be faked. Just as an athlete must invest the long, hard hours of training and must maintain proper diet and conditioning before results are produced, so it is with leadership. To be a good leader you must invest hundreds, even thousands of hours in reading, studying, and applying leadership to be able to master it and become a great leader. In his book *The Outliers*, Malcolm Gladwell refers to what he calls the "10,000-Hour Rule," which states that any given task can be mastered if practiced for about ten thousand hours.

CULTURE TRANSFUSION

If people who don't seem to CARE dominate your current team, you need to look at what *you* might have done as a leader to let it get that way. Did you hire the wrong people? Was there something in your management style that caused them to stop caring over time?

If you hired energized and inspired people but over time they seem to have lost that edge, you may have a chance to change your leadership paradigm in order to win them back. If they had a bad attitude right from the start, you were likely hiring for experience over attitude. One way to fix this may be to let them all go and start over. Just remember that even if you fire everybody and hire a whole new team, unless you change your leadership mindset, you may find yourself right back where you started.

Let's take a look at the way in which we can get full buy-in to our values and principles, so that they truly guide our organization like a constitution, rather than just being meaningless words. We call this method "The 4 In's of Buy-In™".

THE 4 IN'S OF BUY-IN™

Many companies have well-written and well-thought-out values, and yet they struggle to get buy-in from their team. Team members may recite them and even understand them, but they don't live by them.

The 4 In's of Buy-in™ will help you infuse your values and principles into your culture so that they become like a compass guiding everything your company does.

1. INternalize

It all starts with you. Internalization is the first and most important step of instilling the Culture of CARE in your organization. Whether you are a business owner, a team leader, or a new hire, you have a choice to embrace or ignore CARE Leadership principles. We believe that someone who lives according to values and principles earns respect and authority amongst his or her peers. This is called moral authority and can be more influential than the authority that comes from a position or title.

Some of the most influential people in history had no formal title or position, but people listened to them because they earned respect. Gandhi, for instance, helped to free India from British rule, and yet he never held a position in the government. He is known as one of the greatest leaders of all time, and people followed him because he lived his message and led by example.

If we, as CARE Leaders, create a remarkable experience for our team members, then they will do the same for customers. If our team sees that we are having fun and that we love what we do, we will be more successful in instilling the same values in them. Your team will become a reflection of you. If you are sloppy and disorganized, your team will become sloppy and disorganized. If money is your number one priority, it will likely also become the same for your team; they will constantly be looking for a raise, and when your competition offers them more than you are offering, they will leave you high and dry, scrambling for a replacement.

These principles will never take root until you model them and make them your own. To internalize CARE Leadership you have to start thinking like a "CARE Leader" and not as "The Boss." Let's take a look at these two ways of thinking.

The Boss	The CARE Leader
"I look for followers who will do what I tell them to do without asking questions. I do the thinking around here, not them."	"I recruit leaders to my team who question everything, because I recognize that my ideas can be wrong. I value and respect their input."
"I'm the boss. I have the most experience. I make all the decisions. I can't afford to be vulnerable. I need to be seen as the expert on every subject."	"My team is made up of trustworthy leaders at all levels whom I trust to make wise decisions. I trust them because they have character and because I have recruited the best to my team and invested heavily in their skills development."
"I exercise the power of my position to get things done. My philosophy is it's my way or the highway."	"I exercise the power of influence. CARE leadership is about influence built by investing in relationships with my team."
"My employees are here to help me reach my goals."	"I am here to help my team realize their personal and professional goals, in alignment with the company's goals."

The Boss	The CARE Leader
Is self-centered enough to think she has achieved success on her own.

"Who is she to question the way I run my business? I've been at it 30 years, and she just started here."

I keep people at a distance and try to do as much as possible myself. The more people I get involved, the thinner my slice of the pie becomes. | Sees that whatever level of success she has achieved is a result of her dedication and the contributions of the ones around her, and she shows her gratitude often.

"Thanks for the input. I love hearing fresh ideas. As successful as we have been so far, I'm sure there is room for improvement."

The more principled, productive people involved, the bigger the pie can grow. This means more for me and for them. |

2. INtegrate

While "INternalize" deals with your own personal embodiment of the principles, "INtegrate" deals with the way your organization embraces them. There is a subtle but important distinction. Organizations are made up of systems, procedures, and practices that are followed and implemented by the people who work there. When systems and principles are misaligned and not integrated, contradiction occurs between what we say and what we do.

For example:

- We say that we value personal accountability and ownership but implement a system that requires all decisions to be made by the boss.

- Your business values treating people with respect but rewards people exclusively on obtaining financial targets, with little consideration for how people were treated along the way.

- Your company values listening to customers, but you don't have systems in place for customers to make themselves heard.

If you don't integrate systems and principles, just imagine the frustration this causes, not to mention the cynicism and loss of trust that ensues. This is no way to build a great team. Integration must precede inviting great people to your team.

3. INvite

This is a crucial stage in the process of culture building and should come only after the first two stages. Whether you are hiring a new team for the first time or adding to an existing team, it is important to take your time and get it right. This person will either support you in your culture and business building efforts—or work against you.

> If you want motivated people, hire people who are already motivated.

Only invite people to your team who show a strong predisposition to your core principles and values. The more you have internalized these principles, the easier it will be for you to find and invite like-minded people. You will become an expert at asking the right questions and detecting the answers that will reveal the true person you are about to hire. As the saying goes, hire slow and fire fast. This is good advice, and if you do a good job hiring, you shouldn't have to do much firing. Inviting the wrong person can have a devastating effect on your team and on your culture.

> Only invite people to your team who show a strong predisposition to your core principles and values.

For example, someone who doesn't buy in to "don't just do it, own it" will be producing sloppy, inaccurate, or poor-quality work, causing the ones who do take ownership of their duties to have to make up for the slack. This causes resentment in the producers, eventually leading them to believe that your company's principles really aren't that important. If you want motivated people, then hire people who are already motivated. If they aren't, you will not be able to motivate them. You can't change people from who they are; only they can change themselves. Take your time and find the right people before inviting them to your team.

4. INspire

Although motivation and inspiration are very similar in meaning, inspiration refers more to the internal rather than the external. Someone lost in the wilderness may be motivated by hunger to eat a squirrel or a grub, but I doubt they will be inspired to continue the practice once the hunger motivation is satisfied. The word "inspire" comes from the Latin verb *inspirare*, which means "to breathe life into." To inspire others to find their passion and unleash their full potential is your job as a CARE Leader. If you can ignite a fire *within* your team, you will no longer need to light a fire *under* them. "The Boss" mindset looks for ways to extrinsically motivate people; the CARE Leader looks for ways to inspire or intrinsically motivate. Before we can begin to "breathe life into" our team, we must have a good understanding of human motivation. Let's look at the whole-person paradigm and how it helps inspire people to be all that they can be.

CARE LEADERSHIP: A WHOLE-PERSON PARADIGM

In his paper "A Theory of Human Motivation" written in 1943, Abraham Maslow described a theory that he called "the hierarchy of human needs." Maslow discovered that in order for humans to be inspired to achieve greatness, which he called self-actualization, their basic needs must first be met. He found that people have more than just a need to survive; they also want to develop emotionally, mentally, and spiritually. His studies showed that if a basic need was constantly frustrated, then that basic need would became the dominant motivator for that person.

Reading Maslow's theory made me think about all the employees out there who seem to only be motivated by money. Maybe it is because they are always struggling to make ends meet, and as such, getting a raise has become their main motivation. Is it possible that this is why many workers never seem to put their heart, mind, and soul into what they are doing?

Long before I read Maslow's writings I was introduced to this concept throughout my upbringing, and again as a parent. Just imagine you have a newborn baby; what do you need to do first? You need to feed her and provide her with warmth and shelter. But is that where it ends? No, if you want her to grow up happy, secure, and emotionally balanced, then you would need to do more than just feed and shelter her. She will have a better chance of developing to her full potential if she is raised in a secure, loving, caring, and friendly environment, free of bullying and cruelty. This will help her develop emotionally—but not necessarily intellectually. To do that, you need to send her off to school, so she can grow and develop her mind. You must allow her to make mistakes and to learn from them so that she can discover her skills and natural abilities and what she enjoys doing.

And it doesn't end there; there is more to her than just a body, heart, and mind. She also has a spirit that longs for meaning and significance. Your job as a parent is to show her and let her discover that significance and meaning is found by providing value and service to others in a way that lives up to high standards. This regard for the whole person will unleash her potential and sets the conditions needed for achieving greatness.

This understanding applied to a work setting can achieve the same results. The goal for each CARE Leader is to help all team members develop to their full potential. This produces engaged and inspired team members who put not only their bodies, but also their hearts, minds, and souls into their jobs. The result is a highly productive, professional, and passionate workforce. One of our daily operational systems is what we call "The 5 S's of Equipment Care™." We intuitively understand that we must maintain our equipment in order to keep it producing at peak capacity for us. People are no different, and similarly, the "5 S's of Inspiration™" help you "breathe life" into your developing team.

THE 5 S'S OF INSPIRATION™

Businesses can have almost as much impact on a person's life as their family, community, or church. Most of us spend more time at work than we do anywhere else and are therefore heavily influenced by our work environment. To help systematize and integrate the whole-person paradigm, we have developed the 5 S's of Inspiration.

The 5 S's are: Salary (for the body), Security (for the heart), Schooling (for the mind), and Significance and Standards (for the spirit). We developed this hierarchy to illustrate the sequential nature of the 5 S's. Let's begin with Salary.

Salary (for the Body)

Just as with a child, the physiological or survival needs of a team member come first. Team members need to have the wherewithal to feed, clothe, and provide a home for themselves and their families. This can be described as the need for money, and it is at the base of the pyramid, because it must be addressed first. All of the higher levels of the 5S pyramid will collapse if this base need is ignored or neglected. The way a business satisfies this need is through fair and adequate compensation. Fair compensation means that a team member's salary is in line with what other people with the same responsibilities receive at other companies within the industry. It also means that people within your organization aren't being paid unequally for doing the same thing. Adequate compensation means that the team member is earning enough to take care of his or her needs. In addition, team members need to know that through hard work and dedication, they will have the opportunity to advance themselves along a clear career path to make more money.

Once the worry and uncertainty surrounding wages is removed, team members stop thinking about it so much and begin to be inspired to the higher reaches of human achievement. However, if wages are unstable or insufficient and the survival needs of your team are continuously frustrated, you will find that advancement to higher levels of personal growth and contribution will be stifled. When pay is inconsistent or insufficient, team members will feel like they are just barely getting the minimum, and in turn that's all they will give. They will also constantly be looking for a raise or a job elsewhere that pays more.

Proper attention to fair compensation removes money as the sole motivator, allowing a team member to reach for higher inspiration. When salary takes care of the body, the business receives what an able body can produce. Your team members will work hard, do what they are told, and fulfill contractual obligations.

Security (for the Heart)

In the service business, we need people who not only work hard but also genuinely care for our customers and are dedicated to creating a remarkable experience. This requires much more than just their bodies, arms, and backs; it requires an emotional commitment as well. The old song says it right: You've got to have heart!

Our experience is that you cannot simply pay more wages and expect to receive increased loyalty, commitment, care, relationship-building, and respect. Instead, team members must volunteer these qualities. This means that only organizations that understand and look after the needs of the heart are able to unleash the potential of the heart. Team members who feel secure in their jobs, cared for, appreciated, and respected are more likely to respect and show love toward the customers they deal with. One of the greatest longings and needs of the heart is the need for recognition and appreciation. This is missing from many workplaces and causes real insecurity and unhappiness. If we invest in the social, safety, and security needs of the heart, then we can expect team members to put their hearts into their work.

Schooling (for the Mind)

To build a world-class service business you need a world-class team dedicated to continuous improvement and learning. To be profitable and stay ahead of the competition, you require a team that applies their minds to their work. In a school setting, for example, students who feel secure will find their ability to learn greatly increased. The same is true in the workplace.

Most businesses struggle to access the creative and innovative capacity of their teams, resulting in very little buy-in. Innovation becomes driven mostly from the top down. Most initiatives fall flat and never get fully implemented because of a lack of engagement. To get involvement you must make learning an integral part of your culture. Training shouldn't be seen as an event, it has to be a way of life. We will discuss this further in the principle, "Learn something new every day, and share it with the team." Provide ample opportunities for team members to read, study, learn, and apply new things. Invest in professional development and industry certification. Involve team members in research and decision-making that applies to their job. Only then will you be able to unleash their untapped intellectual and creative power. A culture that listens to the ideas put forth by team members creates an exciting and fulfilling place to work. You will begin to attract people who want to develop professionally and become masters of their craft. You will see improvements in every aspect of your business, from operational efficiencies to an improved customer experience—resulting in a better bottom line.

Significance (for the Spirit)

The next aspect pertains to the human spirit. In every human spirit is a deep longing for significance and meaning—for purpose. Your team members need to feel that they are contributing to something bigger than themselves and that they are providing value to others. People want to produce something of value for themselves and for their families. They want to leave a legacy for their children and for their grandchildren.

Just riding a lawn mower or typing data into a spreadsheet day after day may not be enough to produce a sense of fulfillment and purpose. Certainly, one can feel a sense of pride in a job well done or in the joy that their service brings to a customer. But as a team member develops, so does her quest for purpose. Working hard to make the boss wealthy is not enough to inspire greatness in your team; neither is just getting a paycheck. People need to feel a spiritual connection to the mission, vision, and purpose of the organization, one that is worthy of their dedication and commitment. What is your mission? Does it inspire your team and give them purpose?

Standards (for the Spirit)

People who aspire to be world-class in their field need to be a part of something that is also world-class. Organizations with high standards attract people with high standards; they inspire greatness in people. Standards are the conscience of an organization, and they help channel the passion and energy of the team toward the right things. Set the highest standards of ethics, quality, and professionalism for yourself, your company, and your team, and you will begin to attract and retain like-minded team members. In turn, they will set the bar high for themselves and inspire those around them.

∽

As you can see, the 5 S's consider the needs of the whole person: body, heart, mind, and spirit. By focusing on the 5 S's, you inspire team members to offer up their best, often exceeding your expectations and those of your customers.

On the other hand, when companies choose to ignore any of the levels of human inspiration, they can leave employees feeling so unfulfilled at work that they can't wait for the day to end. They can't wait to leave work so they can go elsewhere and do the things that make them happy, that challenge their minds, or that give their lives meaning. They dread Monday morning, and they live for the weekend. Just think of the amazing potential released in organizations that treat team members as whole human beings rather than just bodies to be used and exploited for their labor. Consider the following chart, which illustrates some of the higher manifestations of a whole person in a fulfilling job.

Now that we have a good understanding of the CARE Leadership paradigm and the Culture of CARE, we are ready to begin exploring the eight CARE Leadership principles.

The 5 S's of Inspiration™

The 5 levels	Satisfies	You Provide	Resulting Output
1. Salary	Body	Safe working environment Fair pay Career path	Meeting of contract expectations Endurance Hard work
2. Security	Heart	Culture Financial/Career coaching Recognition Autonomy People CARE systems Relationship with team	 Brand passion Exceeding customer expectations "Second-mile service" Relationship with customers
3. Schooling	Mind	Opportunities to learn and teach Ongoing training Professional development Industry certification	 Vision Competence Trustworthiness Ingenuity Creativity Mastery
4. Significance	Spirit	Triple bottom line Community service Charitable giving	 Purpose Loyality Legacy Conscience Ethical behavior
5. Standards	Spirit	Industry leading: Brand standards systems Quality standards Image standards Ethical standards	 Self-governance Self-motivation CARE leadership Attracting leaders World-class performance

Part 1

CUSTOMERS FIRST

"Taking care of the customer and leaving them happy comes before all else, including making money. As a rule, the money will follow when you do this religiously." —TIM VAN STRALEN

CREATE A REMARKABLE EXPERIENCE
A CULTURE OF WOW!

Today we operate in a hypercompetitive market. Simply providing a good product or service may enable survival, but it will not ensure long-term success. To excel you need to be much more. Companies that learn how to create a remarkable experience for their customers each and every time they deliver a product or service have an advantage in what some have described as the "experience economy."[8]

THE EXPERIENCE ECONOMY

The term "experience economy" is based on the notion that services are beginning to look more and more like commodities. Because of

---

8   The term "experience economy" was coined by B. Joseph Pine II and James H. Gilmore in their book, *The Experience Economy* (Boston: Harvard Business School Press).

the number of competitors in the marketplace, customers have difficulty differentiating one service provider from another. They all seem
to use the same tools and equipment, generally look the same, and
all provide the same quality of service. Whether this is true or not
doesn't matter; perception is reality.

In the absence of any perceived difference in value, then, the
customer will choose the lowest price every time. The only way to
make a sale in this situation is to keep dropping your prices until you
are the lowest. Is this what you want your unique position in the market to be?

If you have ever purchased and used an Apple product you will
have shared in the complete experience that Steve Jobs and his team
worked so hard to create. He obsessed over the experience. Everything from the design of the store or the speed of the website where
you purchased the item shaped your experience—before you ever
opened the box. The ease of opening the packaging and the look and
feel of the product reinforced your emotional connection to your purchase and to the Apple brand.

> "I've learned that people will forget what you said, people will forget
> what you did, but people will never forget how you made them feel."
>
> —Maya Angelou

Apple knew that just having a phone that worked wouldn't be
good enough; all phones on the market work well. Image, design,
quality, functionality, and exceptional customer service all combine
to create a customer experience that has become legendary. The result
is an almost cult-like following. People line up outside for days to be

among the first to experience new Apple products as they are released into the market.

For you to thrive in today's marketplace, of course you must offer a great product or flawless service. But then, your customers have to be left with a good feeling about the experience they've had with your company. It is this feeling that forms their perception of your brand.

Three components are required for you to thrive in the experience economy: be different, be remarkable, and be consistent.

1. BE DIFFERENT

To stand out in a crowded marketplace you have to be noticeably different from your competition. Our family started in the landscape maintenance business, an industry with a low barrier to entry and low starting capital requirement. This encourages many new start-ups to enter the marketplace each year. They operate with little overhead and offer their services at low prices. At first this caused us concern, but we quickly learned how to use this situation to our advantage.

Since it was easy to get into the industry, the market became populated with unreliable, untrained, and unprofessional competitors. We were able to stand out in the marketplace by exceeding customer expectations. Perceptions can be more powerful than reality, so we set about discovering what the perception of the landscaping industry was in the minds of our customers. This was so critical that we didn't want to leave it to guesswork, so we asked a lot of questions. Informally, we asked people what their frustrations were with the industry and why they were planning to switch service providers.

What we heard was that poor service quality and low professionalism were big problems. Many companies were operating with unreliable equipment operated by shady-looking employees. They were rushing through their jobs and cutting corners—delivering substandard service.

People told us that pricing appeared opportunistic and unpredictable. Despite the low prices, people were still feeling gouged. They wanted to pay fair yet competitive prices. They weren't satisfied with the value they were receiving.

Commercial clients in particular complained that contractors would perform work without proper protective equipment and operate in an unsafe manner. They were looking for a contractor who was dedicated to ongoing training and safety.

We also heard that reliability was virtually nonexistent in the industry. Clients would say, "I can't rely on my landscaper. They don't show up when they say they will, and they are never available when I try to contact them. When I leave a message, they take forever to get back to me."

Lastly, we heard that customers wanted a service provider who subscribed to and made an effort toward the use of environmentally sustainable practices. There is a growing priority within our target customers for green products and services.

Once we collected the data, we used it to analyze our existing service offering. What emerged from our analysis was a system we call SCORE™. It stands for:

- **S**ervice Quality and Professionalism;

- **C**ompetitive and Fair Pricing;

- **O**ngoing Training and Safety;

- **R**eliable Service and Communications;

- **E**nvironmental and Social Sustainability

Next we wrote out our unique marketplace differences in a way that could be memorized and easily recited when asked. "What makes you different from all the other companies out there?" is by far the question we get asked the most. Here's what we tell them:

Clean, shiny trucks

Friendly, uniformed personnel

Three-hour call-back guarantee

State-of-the-art equipment, sharpened daily

Quality-control reports, delivered monthly

Each of our five key differences is backed up by a system that ensures their consistent delivery. Internally, we call these our five promises.

> "We are what we repeatedly do. Excellence, therefore, is not an act but a habit."
>
> —Aristotle

The habitual use of these systems ensures that they are implemented consistently. They have been "institutionalized" in the way we operate—part of our DNA. These systems help us to create a remarkable experience for our customers. They allow us to compete at a world-class level, affording us the opportunity to solicit a more discerning customer.

2. BE REMARKABLE

One way to be remarkable is to go above and beyond the expectations of your customers. Let me share a remarkable experience that I've had. A few years ago my wife and I attended a leadership conference that took place on a Royal Caribbean cruise ship, *The Jewel of the Sea*. Each day we attended meetings and training sessions in various conference rooms throughout the ship. While we were out, the cleaning staff would clean our room—this is the basic level of service we would have expected. If we had returned to find the room in the same condition as when we left it that morning, we would have not only been disappointed, but also we might have called the front desk to complain. If the cleaning staff did a great job, as was expected, the service probably would have gone unnoticed.

However, the team working on *The Jewel of the Sea* understands that in order to inspire passengers to share their experiences, the crew and staff have to be remarkable and give more than is expected.

They have taught their cleaning team how to fold towels creatively into little animals. This cost them nothing other than a few extra minutes of their time . . . but it did help to create a remarkable experience!

I've told lots of people about this experience and showed them these pictures of the little dog and the elephant that they folded and left in the cabin room to greet us when we returned. This small gesture was an excellent example of a team

member doing something out of the ordinary to enhance a guest's overall experience.

In our line of business, our customers don't come to us; we go to them. So, if our teams arrive at a customer's property and the garbage cans or recycle bins are down by the road, then the team brings them up to the garage. If an irrigation technician is going into a customer's house, he will slip on a pair of boot covers to show respect and care for the customer's flooring.

We take ownership and do whatever it takes to make customers feel important. We may get a coffee for a guest or make sure we greet them at the door. Maybe it's sending a handwritten note to say "thank you." No one needs to ask permission before going the extra mile. Every team member has a budgeted "culture fund" expense line and is free to spend it as needed. Often, of course, the best experiences are from the heart and cost little or nothing to create.

Doing something extraordinary to create a remarkable experience for our customers makes them feel special—like a guest at a high-end resort. When customers feel special, you earn their loyalty. When the experience is remarkable, they talk about it to their friends and colleagues. But what happens if we are inconsistent? Inconsistency confuses and eventually alienates the customer. So . . .

3. BE CONSISTENT

Consider this scenario: Susan Smith hires us to cut her lawn because she has heard so much about us from a friend. She is also really looking for a change from the unreliable and unprofessional people who currently perform the service; she doesn't feel comfortable around them. After hearing about The Grounds Guys from her friend she says to herself, "Friendly, uniformed personnel; clean, shiny trucks. I have got to see this."

The first day of service is on Monday, so she makes sure that she is home to see the team arrive and mow her lawn. Sure enough, the team arrives as scheduled. They park on the road. As promised, the truck is "clean and shiny," gleaming with professionalism and quality. The team gets out in full uniform, smiles and waves to her as she sips her coffee on the front porch, and immediately begins their work. "Wow!" she says. "This is a real treat!" One team member picks up the garbage bins that had been emptied and are sitting upside down at the end of the driveway and carries them up to the garage. The team goes about their duties in a safe and professional manner, and it seems like everybody knows exactly what they need to do. The team finishes the service, leaving her property smelling like freshly mowed grass and looking amazing. Every detail was looked after and she can see the team leader doing a final inspection while the rest of the team loads up the equipment. "Great job!" she says as they leave.

"That was an amazing experience. I've got to tell somebody about this. I wonder who Mom uses at her condo? She's on the board of directors there. I'll give her a call," she thinks to herself.

Susan's mother is not thrilled with the people who manage the property at her condo and complains that they are unreliable. Susan invites her mom to come over for coffee on Monday morning and to enjoy The Grounds Guys experience.

I think you can see where this is going. What happens if the team that shows up on Monday is inconsistent in their approach? What if this time they skipped washing the truck because they didn't feel like it? What if a few team members wore jeans or were in a bad mood and didn't smile or wave? What if they left the garbage cans this time and just kicked them aside?

Inconsistency kills trust and makes liars out of everyone making brand promises. It damages the reputation of your brand. You can't afford it.

Part 2

ATTITUDE

If you can ignite a fire within *them, you will not need to keep lighting a*
fire under *them.*

HAVE FUN AND LOVE WHAT YOU DO
A CULTURE OF PASSION!

"Your work is going to fill a large part of your life, and the only way to be truly satisfied is to do what you believe is great work. And the only way to do great work is to love what you do!" —**STEVE JOBS**

Having fun and loving what you do is an important part of our culture. In fact, many great leaders would say that it is their secret to success. Being a leader is not easy. If it were, everyone would do it. Anyone who has attained a high level of success in anything will tell you that success only comes through hard work.

Read about Thomas Edison, Michael Jordan, or Steve Jobs. These leaders attained success only after experiencing many failures and putting in many hours of hard work. As leaders and business builders, we often find ourselves in challenging situations that require us to step out of our comfort zone. We also know that being in business for ourselves or working for a progressive, entrepreneurial company can be very rewarding. If viewed with the right attitude, it can be a lot of fun, too.

CHANGE WHAT YOU LOVE

Stepping out of our comfort zone to do the things that we don't like to do—or may even fail at—is not fun, but it is the only way to grow. In business, when you find yourself comfortable and cozy, you are in grave danger of becoming extinct. This is a fast-paced world. What worked ten or even five years ago may be obsolete today. Our minds are programmed to interpret discomfort as pain, so we avoid it at all costs. Change is uncomfortable so we remain stagnant. To be successful in business and to have fun (despite the discomfort) we have to reprogram our thinking. We need to see discomfort as our path to growth and learning. We must embrace the feeling and push ourselves out of our comfort zone.

> "You either suffer the pain of discipline or the pain of regret."
>
> —Pinball Clemons

A few years ago my brothers and I hired a personal trainer to help us get into shape. At first I resented the way he pushed us; my body ached all over! But after a while I began to see results: I had more energy and I felt great. I learned to love the soreness in my shoulders and arms, because I knew it was making me stronger. I recall leaving on a business trip that prevented me from going to the gym. After a day on the road I began to notice something missing: the soreness in my arms. I started getting up early to jog and do push-ups to bring back the sensation of worked muscles that I had learned to love.

"If you love what you do, you'll never work a day in your life."

—Confucius

Have you ever had to get up and speak in front of a group of strangers? Do you remember how you felt? Remember the knot in your stomach, the sweaty palms, the dryness in your mouth? Train yourself to love that feeling; this is a prerequisite to growth. Once you eagerly welcome the chance to experience life outside of your comfort zone, what was once pain becomes fun—and what was comfortable becomes the pain of an opportunity lost. If you want to have fun and love what you do, then learn to love the challenges that you face in your business. Without challenges and discomfort there is no growth. And if you're not growing, you're going backwards.

MAKE TIME FOR FUN

Having fun at work is so important that you have to make time for it and *make it happen*. I'm not sure how this tradition got started, but we had a lot of fun fitting everyone who worked for us with a nickname. After a while a name would appear that suited a team member, and it would stick. They weren't always flattering names, but if the team member liked it—or at least didn't protest too much—the name would catch on, and that was it. Names like Pirate, Crusty the Clown, Happy, Sleepy, Grey, Middle, Whitey, Jacket, The New Guy, and The New Guy's Brother would be used so exclusively that even their own parents started using them. Middle, for example, always sat in the center seat of the truck, and Jacket wore his uniform jacket even on the hottest days of the summer. What really surprised us was that he also wore only the same jacket in the frigid winter months. One fellow's nickname was Wormy, not because he had worms, but probably because of his willingness to get in the dirt and "get-r-done." He is still working for the company, sixteen years later. This became a real source of fun at work, except maybe for people in the payroll office, who would receive pay records with nicknames on them and reply, "I don't see any 'Pirates' in the system."

Years later I was volunteering at our local fire hall and a gentleman came up and introduced himself to me. With a big smile on his face he said, "Hi, I'm Whitey's dad." He went on to say that his son, who had worked for us while going to college, was now married with a few children. He said Whitey speaks fondly of the years he worked for us and said that the values he learned have helped him not only in his professional life but also as a father.

We also took time every summer to have what we call "Sunshine Day." It's a day where we shut down operations and take everybody off to do something fun, like paintball, go-cart racing, or even wakeboarding at the lake. Paintball was always a favorite, and our team members would eagerly look forward to Sunshine Day. To make it fun we would set up paintball teams: van Stralens against the team members. This worked well until one year we realized our company had grown too big for that arrangement. Fifty against ten was bad odds, and my brothers and I got shot up pretty bad. As we nursed our bruises we thought of other games we could play that would be less painful. Today Sunshine Day has become a tradition practiced by all of our locations to let team members know that we value and appreciate them. We think it's important to have fun and love what you do.

A GREATER PURPOSE

I heard a story when I was young that I have thought about many times since. It illustrates the difference that purpose and vision can make, and it goes something like this:

Back in the days of ancient Rome, a traveler came upon a group of workers chipping away at stones beside the road. He asked one of the workers, who seemed to be angrily pounding away at the stones, what are you working on? The angry worker replied with a frown, "I'm chipping stones." A little farther down the road the traveler noticed another worker who was singing happily as he worked. "What are you doing?" he asked the happy worker. The man smiled and replied, "I am building a temple."

What caused the difference in attitude? I think the story illustrates the fact that if you have a vision or a greater purpose in mind, you look at your job with a different perspective. Someone once said, "We don't see things as they are; we see them as we are." If we change our thinking, the whole situation can change. Both of the workers in the story were doing the same job, but the happy one, the one who was having fun and loving his job, was the one who had a vision—a clear purpose.

It's important to be clear about this principle. Some may ask, "Are you suggesting that if I love hockey, I should go out and try to earn my living as a hockey player? Or if I love playing guitar, I should join a band and bank my family's future on the hopes that I'll be a rock star?" The answer is no—not unless it is your life's dream and ambition and you love it so much that you are willing to invest the blood, sweat, tears, time, and hard work that is required for success. Not unless you love it so much that even if you never became a successful musician you'd still have fun along the way and wouldn't see the time wasted. Any successful musician will tell you that "overnight" success came after many years of practice and hard work. Numerous times they were tempted to give up as they played to only five or six people, wondering where their next meal was going to come from. Success comes from forming good habits and doing those small, seemingly insignificant things consistently over an extended period of time.

The true spirit behind this principle is to find meaning and fulfillment in what you are doing *right now*. Find the real purpose for what you do and for what your business does. Although the reason any for-profit business exists is to make money, that usually isn't enough to sustain you through the difficult times. If your only purpose for work is to make money, then you won't last—period. People whose energy, excitement, ambition, and drive come from money alone are in for a roller-coaster ride of emotions. When times are good, their spirits are high, but when times are tough and money is short, their spirits are low. Soon they are ready to throw in the towel. They begin to lose their love for what they do, and their team sees it. Before long they are looking for a new team.

When your team, customers, vendors, and colleagues see that you are enjoying life in the process, they will be attracted to you and to your business. Everything will change for the better. Sales and team-building will become easier, and success will follow!

Life is a journey, not a destination. You need to enjoy life *right now*, in the job you are in *right now*, in the financial situation you are in *right now*. If your only motivator is money, then no amount will ever be enough. You will always be unhappy with your current situation. Life is too short; don't spend it waiting for the day that your ship comes in! Your ship is in; it's right here, waiting for you to make the most of it. It's time to enjoy life in the process!

What is your greater purpose? Is it to run a world-class business that brings structure and order to the lives of your team and your family? Could it be to build a business based on values that helps improve the lives of everyone your company comes into contact with? Could you enhance the lives of your customers, vendors, and team members by what they experience from your business? Can you use your workforce to give back to those in need?

Can you use your business to help spread the message of CARE to everyone you come into contact with, to leave a lasting and positive impression? In a world of negativity and bad news, can you and your company be a beacon on a hill, a shining light of hope for all who come into contact with you? What if the values you teach and live every day in your business helped others to be better parents, spouses, sons, or daughters? What impact do you think you as a leader can have on the lives around you?

The challenge of making a difference in the world sounds like fun to me! That sounds like something anyone can love to do, like something that can sustain you through the difficult times and the mundane tasks that you will find yourself doing. Get a vision for that, and you will breathe new life into your day. You will find renewed energy and strength to get you through the tough times. You will no longer be waiting for "someday when . . ." You will no longer be just putting in time. You will be making a difference and building an empire of CARE that will allow you to have fun and love what you do!

DON'T JUST DO IT—OWN IT!
A CULTURE OF ACCOUNTABILITY

There are two ways to do anything. One way is to do it without putting much thought or care into your task. Another is to take full responsibility for the professional completion of your task and, as we like to say, "own it!" When you are looking for team members to contribute positively to your team, look for people who demonstrate a clear understanding of commitment and accountability. Look for and recruit people who can demonstrate that they care about their work.

Have you ever asked someone to type out a document for you, and when you got it back, it was full of spelling errors and sentences that don't make sense? Can you imagine the impact on your business if your bookkeeper entered income and payment information in an inaccurate and haphazard manner? Team members who live by "Don't Just Do It—Own It!" go out of their way to make sure that the work they do is performed to the highest standards. They take ownership of the task and are proud to call it their own: they OWN it.

If this principle is rarely seen in your team, you will be forced to become a micromanager. You may have to redo tasks that you have hired someone else to do. This situation has a crippling effect on your ability to grow as a person, as a department, or as a company. Your time as a leader is best spent doing the things that will build your business. These activities include networking, marketing, building relationships, inspiring, training, and driving culture within your organization. In order to be free to do these activities, you need to have the right team in place. Team members must be responsible for their role within your organization, and they need to take complete ownership of it. Let's take a look at the ways in which you can create the type of culture that allows for this principle to take root in your organization—the culture that gets results.

THE "I HAVE NO TIME" VICIOUS CYCLE

When the "Don't Just Do It—Own It" principle is absent, you run the risk of getting bogged down in what I like to call the "I Have No Time" Vicious Cycle. I often speak with small business owners who are caught in this cycle. They know what needs to be done to fix the problem, but they simply can't find time to do it. I ask why they have no time, and the answer is almost always, "I'm too busy running around putting out fires." They complain that their team is incompetent and requires constant monitoring. Team members do their job in a careless, slipshod manner, and supervisors are forced to retrace their steps and redo their work properly. "If I want the job done right, I have to do it myself," they say.

This situation soon becomes a cycle that owners cannot escape.

The busier they become, the less time there is to build, develop, and lead their company. And the less the owner works to build, develop, and lead the team, the less time she has! After all, the "I Have No Time" Vicious Cycle is caused by the absence of people who "own it." Here are three steps for infusing "Don't Just Do It—Own It!" into your culture so that you can break free from the vicious cycle.

1. Decide

Step one is for you to make the decision to stop the vicious cycle. A decision is not a wish list; it is a commitment to change. A true decision is made evident through your words and actions. Replace the words "We would like to . . ." with "We will . . . !" Once you've made the decision to implement a change, you will need to remove any thoughts of failure and focus completely on success. A technique that I have found to be helpful is visualization: the skill of visualizing the end result of your decision as if it has already happened.

Take a minute to close your eyes and imagine what your business looks like once you have achieved your stated goal. Look a year into the future and write down what you see. What does your day look like at work and at home? What do your customers say about you? Visualize your team. What do they look like and how do they feel about their job?

Once you have a clear picture, write it down in the affirmative. Use sentences like, "Our customer loyalty score is consistently 95 percent or higher," "Our customers speak highly of us," and "Word-of-mouth advertising is our number-one source of new business." Whatever you want to have happen, visualize it and then write it down.

Remember when you were learning how to drive a car? Your instructor told you not to focus on the ditch, but rather to focus on staying on the road. If all you can think about is "avoid the ditch, avoid the ditch," you are likely to end up in it! Whatever you focus on you will get more of, so focus on what you want to happen, and you will achieve it.

In the book *Double Double*, Cameron Herold describes a visualization technique that he calls "The Painted Picture." This technique involves leaning forward through an imaginary wall, three years into the future. Mark Wardell from Wardell Professional Development is another business advisor who helps his clients with a similar visualization method called a "Strategic Vision." Jim Collins, author of *Good to Great*, has a concept that he calls BHAG, which stands for "Big, Hairy, Audacious Goal." We have used each of these visualization techniques in our business and can attest to their prophetic power. Your visualization now becomes a unifying goal that you will share with your team on a regular basis, giving substance and clarity to your decision.

Your decision must also be absolute. I once read that when conquistador Hérnan Cortés arrived in South America, he burned his ships, removing any chance for him or his people to go back. This is the mindset that is required. Your team will feed off of your determination and commitment. Anthony Robins says, "Decision is the father of all action." As a leader, you will have to be clear on what you want to achieve and be committed to doing whatever it takes to get it. Every decision produces an outcome, and deciding to do nothing will not break the "I have no time" cycle. Once you make the decision to change, it's time to take action.

When Cortés reached the New World he burned his ships—as a result, his men were well motivated.

2. Interrupt the Cycle

The second step is to stop the wheel from spinning out of control. You need to interrupt or disrupt the patterns and habits that are causing the vicious cycle. In order to stop a regular repeating pattern, something irregular and unexpected has to occur. One way to interrupt the cycle might be to draw up a banner that says

Under New Management

. . . and hang it where your team will see it first thing on Monday morning. Your team will be curious and ask questions. This is your opportunity to share your decision with your team. Once you have your team's attention, you can reassure them that you didn't sell your business or hire a new manager, but that you are going to start leading in a new way; the normal way of doing things is going to change. New systems will be implemented one-by-one that will help the entire team be more efficient, more organized, and less stressed. Read your vision or painted picture to the team and ask them for their input and feedback. The more clearly they see the same vision as you, the more likely they are to help you achieve it.

> "Without involvement, there is no commitment. Mark it down, asterisk it, circle it, underline it. No involvement, no commitment."
> —Stephen R. Covey

Let your team know that in order to achieve your vision, you are going to require a full commitment from everyone. You are going to require each individual to look at his or her job in a new way. They can no longer just do it—they will need to OWN it! Ask them if they are okay with that.

Most if not all of your team will be on board. People don't enjoy working in a vicious cycle; it's stressful on everyone, and stress is a morale buster. If your team sees that you are trying to bring some order into their lives and to make their day more enjoyable, they will be on board.

I know from my own experience that I am far more likely to take ownership of an idea if it was my own or if I was involved in developing it, as compared to having it imposed upon me. CARE Leadership is about moving away from the outdated, top-down, authoritarian leadership style of a bygone era towards a leadership style where everyone's contribution and involvement is encouraged. CARE Leaders involve everyone in their continuous-improvement planning, from the minimum-wage team member to the senior executive.

It may be a hard truth to accept, but the reason your company got into a vicious cycle in the first place was because of YOU. Perhaps you hired improperly, or didn't take time to train and develop leaders, or didn't demonstrate a real commitment to systemization. The bad news is that YOU are the problem. The good news is that YOU are also the solution!

3. Pick One: Install a New Habit / Procedure / System

Step three is to "Pick One." This means choosing a system or habit that you believe will produce the most significant results in the shortest amount of time. Choose a system that will eliminate some of the time wasters that are causing the "I Have No Time" vicious cycle. Make sure you solicit feedback from your team when choosing your "pick one."

For example, if you find yourself continuously delivering parts, fuel, or supplies to your teams in the field, then you may want to develop a checklist system to ensure that each vehicle is fully stocked and equipped with enough parts and tools to handle any scenario a team might run into during their daily route.

If you are spending three hours a week delivering parts to your teams, then implementing this system could save you 150 hours over the course of a year. That's almost a month! Just think of how your business could improve if you had an extra 150 hours of time to work on it.

BEST PRACTICE

It's best to implement one new system at a time. Allow time for the system to become a habit before moving on to the next. A system cannot accomplish what it was designed for until it becomes ingrained in your company routine and is delegated properly to the right people.

Common traits of successful entrepreneurs are that they are ambitious, driven, and committed. Entrepreneurs are the embodiment of the principle "Don't Just Do It—Own It!" Their drive and ambition empowers them to learn every aspect of their business and to master it. They know their customers, services, and products better than anyone. They can execute their systems better than anyone. While this is the reason for their initial success, it ultimately becomes a limiting factor somewhere down the road. At some point every entrepreneur reaches his or her limit and becomes "maxed out." Many small businesses simply stop growing at this point.

Companies that grow beyond this "glass ceiling" and find a way to take it to the next level are the ones that learn how to transfer everything they know to someone else. I've heard a business owner exclaim, "If I could clone myself, I'd be able to double my business!" Well, the reality is that you *can* clone yourself. A true CARE Leader's goal should be to develop as many competent leaders as possible within the organization. Every time you help to build another leader, you extend your capacity for growth.

A great place to start is by learning the art of proper delegation. My brothers and I learned an effective method of delegation while training to fly a helicopter. Just like running a business or department, there are many components to flying a helicopter. We started with the easiest stuff, like straight and level flight. Then we moved on to hovering, landing, takeoff, confined spaces, and so on. Each time we were to learn a different skill, our instructor would first demonstrate the skill, then he would observe us performing the skill, and finally we would fly solo, using the skill. During each phase, we spent countless hours practicing until the pilot instructor was confident that we were ready for the next step.

Cutting corners in a helicopter can cost you your life. Cutting corners in the delegation process can cost you a customer, money, or your business. Let's take a look at how we can apply a simple, three-step delegation process that we call "proper delegation" to your organization. Just as in our helicopter flight training, the three steps are 1) demonstrate, 2) observe, and 3) solo.

PROPER DELEGATION

I once read an article that put forth the idea that everyone in your organization should be the CEO of his or her job. As chief executive officers of the jobs or departments, they need to have the attitude,

"The buck stops here. I am fully responsible for my role in this company. If things go wrong, I take responsibility and I fix it."

This can be a team member responsible for edging gardens at a customer's property or an administrative assistant entering data into a software program. In either case, the team member needs to commit to the role and own it. Once they have received training, practiced, and have developed confidence, team members can begin making decisions within their area of responsibility without having to rely on input from you.

But let's back up a minute. Before you can ask a team member to be a CEO of his or her role, both you and your team member will need to be very clear on what that role is. A great way to do this is to ask your team member in a casual, one-on-one conversation what he understands his role to be. Compare his understanding with your expectations and build a list together of mutually agreed-upon roles and responsibilities. By including your team member in the discussion, you begin the process of buy-in, a necessary requirement for a team member to "own" the job. Without clarity, your team members will be dependent on you for constant direction.

Once all team members are clear on their responsibilities, you must provide training so they can complete their tasks. If you have recruited a team member with a positive and helpful attitude, then you should have no problem training her for the duties at hand.

The next thing you need to do is to provide the guidelines within which your team member can operate. What decisions can they make without your input? What decisions require your approval? You will need to revisit these guidelines from time to time to maintain clarity.

Let's use a real-world example from The Grounds Guys. Imagine you have hired a service technician who seems to be a culture fit and who has demonstrated sufficient technical competency to complete his tasks. You have a young family at home and need the freedom to be able to end your day earlier than your team. To delegate your end-of-day closing procedures, I would suggest you follow these three steps of "proper delegation":

1. Demonstrate: This step can take anywhere from one to two weeks, depending on the team member and the complexity of the task. For this particular scenario, you need to be present each day during the closing procedures. For the first day or two you demonstrate the proper way of doing things to your trainee while explaining the reasons behind each task. When you are confident that your trainee understands both the how and the why, you can proceed to step two.

2. Observe: Allow your team member to demonstrate the task for you. Follow the team member through the procedure and ensure he is performing the tasks correctly. Ask him to complete each task while explaining its importance. Remember, CARE Leaders build other CARE Leaders. You need to invest time in your team members in order for them to become CARE Leaders. Don't cut corners. Someday you may rely on this person to train other new recruits, and you want to be certain that they know the system. Begin stage three only when you are comfortable that the team member can perform the task consistently and at the expected quality level.

3. Solo: For the final step you must allow your team member to fly solo. Be nearby and accessible the first time he performs the tasks on his own, but do not get involved. If everything runs smoothly, then after a day or two you can inform your team member that you won't be present, but you are available by phone if he has any questions. Attend the procedure every

other day for a week or two to confirm the job is being done properly. When you are confident that your team member has mastered the system, step three is complete!

Congratulations! You have successfully delegated a task or system to your team member. You have set him up for success and have provided the tools required to not just do it, but to own it! By allowing a team member to handle a task that you once had to manage or even do yourself, you have freed up your time for business development, customer relationship building, or spending time with your family. The three steps of "proper delegation" can be repeated for any task or duty within your operating system. The time frame of each of the stages will vary with the complexity of the task.

THE REGULAR REVIEW

To ensure that the delegated tasks continue to run smoothly, you must commit to a regular review. We do this by conducting a daily morning huddle. During the huddle we review and discuss the activities of the previous day. This is your opportunity as a leader to make sure everything went well the day before. You will also use this opportunity to discuss any challenges, ideas, or suggestions your team members have.

> "Few things can help an individual more than to place responsibility on him, and to let him know that you trust him."
>
> —Booker T. Washington

"Don't Just Do It—Own it" is an attitude as much as it is a principle. It is an important component of the Culture of CARE. If you continue to embed this principle in your culture, you will eventually remove yourself from day-to-day operations. This is not a luxury—it is a requirement for the growth and sustainability of your business.

Two more components are key to the success of instilling "Don't Just Do It—Own It" within your company. Without these critical two components you will sabotage your own efforts and destroy the confidence and morale of your team. The final two components are communication and trust.

Many entrepreneurs have a difficult time trusting others to do their job. For this principle to take root and remain strong you will have to stay out of the way and give your team members the authority and autonomy required to do their job. After following the three steps of proper delegation and completely handing over ownership of the task, do not interfere. This doesn't mean that you should abandon your team . . . it simply means that you should refrain from micro-managing them. Your involvement at this point is to assist in any way they require and to provide them with the resources and support they need to be successful. Nothing kills "Don't Just Do It—Own It" faster than when a team member's decisions are undermined or overridden by superiors. We will discuss trust and trustworthiness in detail in connection with the principle "Be Ethical and Trustworthy in Your Dealings." People with enough intelligence and ambition to "own" their roles and responsibilities won't function under micromanagement. They will be chased away, leaving behind a group of people who take orders without thinking for themselves.

BE HUMBLE
A CULTURE OF "WE"

"The best leaders in our research display tremendous ambition for their company combined with the stoic will to do whatever it takes, no matter how brutal (within the bounds of the company's core values), to make the company great. Yet at the same time they display a remarkable humility about themselves, ascribing much of their own success to luck, discipline, and preparation rather than personal genius."

—JIM COLLINS, AUTHOR OF *GOOD TO GREAT*

Humility is a simple yet often misunderstood principle. And yet it is at the core of what makes CARE Leadership work. I am convinced that this principle, when properly understood and applied, is the secret to developing real and meaningful relationships with the people on your team. Meaningful relationships are essential to building the Culture of CARE within an organization. In the dictionary, humility is defined as "the state or quality of being not proud or haughty"[9] or as "modest opinion or estimate of one's own importance."[10] I have divided this principle into five key components:

1. The Boss vs. The CARE Leadership Paradigm
2. Putting the Needs of our Customers and Colleagues First
3. Humility leads by Example
4. Humility causes you to be Thankful
5. Humility helps us to be more Teachable

Each component contributes in its own unique way to the tapestry of CARE Leadership. Let's take a look at them, one at a time.

1. THE BOSS VS. THE CARE LEADERSHIP PARADIGM

Every leader starts as "the boss." That means that you started a business or someone has promoted you to lead a team, project, or department. Your so-called power or influence comes from your title. Your team does what you tell them to do because they have to. After all, you're the boss.

Some people see a title or position as an indication that they have "arrived." Instead, view it as the starting point for your growth as a leader. John C. Maxwell said, "Being a boss does not make you a leader, but being a leader can make you a great boss." Unfortunately, many bosses fail to grow into true leaders, perhaps because they don't realize that in order to rise in leadership you must diminish in self-importance. Exercising your power as "the boss" without building

---

9   *Merriam-Webster* website, s.v. "humble," http://www.merriam-webster.com /dictionary/humble.

10   Dictionary.com, s.v. "humility," http://dictionary.reference.com/browse /humility?s=t.

true relationships is not a long-term strategy for success. It can be fast and easy to gain compliance by threatening someone's job, but the compliance doesn't last. People will do what you demand only until they can find a better place to work; then they move on. You will churn through team members until no one wants to work for you except for those who have no better options. There is no real power in a position, because people with drive and ambition always have the freedom to go elsewhere.

CARE Leaders, on the other hand, look at their organizations as a vehicle through which all team members can achieve their personal and professional goals. This attitude helps to unleash the energy and ambition of everyone on your team. No longer are team members just punching the clock and blindly obeying your commands. They are learning and looking for ways to do things better. The whole company improves as more leaders are attracted to your team. When you put the needs of your team ahead of your own and show genuine care for them, they give you their permission to lead them. This is a key difference between the boss and the CARE Leader. People follow you because they want to, not because they have to. Leaders who earn this level of trust unleash the power of people. Imagine the results when your team is empowered, self-motivated, and energetic in their work. What is the effect on your bottom line when team members are contributing their creativity and enthusiasm, rather than just counting down the hours until quitting time?

2. PUTTING THE NEEDS OF OUR CUSTOMERS AND COLLEAGUES FIRST

Humility allows us to be hard on the system and soft on the people; it helps us put the needs of our customers first by enabling us to see things from their perspective. It allows us to admit when we make a mistake and set it right. The systems that we developed in our company have come from mistakes that caused us to either lose money or lose a customer.

> "Humility does not mean you think less of yourself. It means you think of yourself less."
>
> —Ken Blanchard

We would immediately look at our mistake, identify the reason it happened, and implement a system to prevent it from ever happening again. A humble mindset allows us to acknowledge that we do make mistakes and we are not too proud to admit it. A simple, sincere apology is much more effective at resolving a customer issue than a defensive response or an excuse. I have seen potentially heated issues defused immediately by a humble apology and immediate action to resolve the issue. Humility is not weakness nor is it a lack of the passionate pursuit of personal or professional goals. Humility is being proud of who you are and your achievements without arrogance; it is about continually recognizing the contributions of others while shifting the focus away from yourself. Humility is about trying to help others—but it is not necessarily about trying to make everyone happy. There are times when you will have to make tough decisions that will not please everyone. You will earn the respect of your team when you make those decisions guided by your principles.

3. HUMILITY LEADS BY EXAMPLE

We all know that people learn more from what we do than from what we say. I recall reading a story about the legendary leadership of Walt

Disney. He had declared that a key difference at Disney Theme Parks was that they would be clean and free of trash. To keep this promise, they hired more custodial staff than their competitors and trained everyone to keep an eye open for litter.

One day Walt Disney was observed picking up a small piece of trash off the ground and putting it into his pocket. A supervisor came over to him and said, "Mr. Disney, you don't need to do that. We have staff to do that work. You must have more important things to do."

Walt replied, "No one has more important work to do than to keep our promises." If Walt Disney had been the type of proud leader that refused to get into the trenches with his team and lead by example, his company would not be what it is today. We've all heard the truism: "Truths are caught, not taught." As leaders, and collectively as a company, we must live our values or risk having them become just meaningless words.

4. HUMILITY CAUSES YOU TO BE THANKFUL

The boss doesn't feel like he needs to be thankful for team members; he thinks in terms of "what are my people costing me" rather than celebrating their contribution to the company. The boss worries: "If I show them too much appreciation, they will come asking for a raise."

This worry is not an issue when you have a great culture and a clear career path set up, where pay increases are attached to learning and contribution. The real issue is that it takes humility to recognize the contributions of others and to thank them for their efforts. Genuine thankfulness helps to eliminate the "us vs. them" mentality that plagues most organizations. In many small businesses, it's "The Boss vs. The Employees." In a family business it can be "The Family vs. The Employees." In a franchise system it can be "Franchisees vs.

the Franchisor." Growth at many companies is stifled because of this destructive and counterproductive way of thinking. And it all comes from a lack of humility. It stems from people looking out solely for their own interests instead of the interests of others.

When you achieve success as a company or an individual, humility helps you see it all from the right perspectives. The following excerpt is from a story written in a past issue of the *Landscape Ontario Magazine*.

Thankful
Contributed by Tony DiGiovanni,
Executive Director of Landscape Ontario

Sometimes one word speaks volumes.

Recently, Allen Denis (Editor of *Horticulture Review*) and I had a wonderful opportunity to visit the Sunshine home office . . . The moment I entered the building I could sense this was a special place. The television screen in the lobby displayed a greeting: "Welcome Allan and Tony from Landscape Ontario."

The tour started in the café where I met a number of other brothers and staff. We talked about their history, company philosophy, and operations. The business is based on a very simple philosophy of passion for service and sincere CARE for customers, employees, and community. Tim and his brother Peter described their aspirations, company vision, employee philosophy, and the need for balancing family, business, and spiritual life. Employees are encouraged and recognized when they provide unexpected and special customer service . . .

I could not help feeling a little proud that Tim was one of my students and that The Grounds Guys is a member of the Landscape

Ontario community. As I was leaving, I turned to Tim's father, Fred van Stralen, and said, "You must be very proud of your children."

Without hesitation he replied, "I am very thankful." That one word made a huge and positive impression. I imagine that Fred's "thankful" attitude has influenced the Sunshine and van Stralen life journey. It certainly influenced me.

Being thankful reduces fear and uncertainty. In our increasingly fast-paced and insecure world, thankfulness stimulates positive thoughts and feelings. It reveals our blessings. It provides hope. It encourages and supports. It grounds us. Thanks, Fred.

5. HUMILITY HELPS US BE MORE TEACHABLE

Just the act of studying and learning is humbling in itself, as Albert Einstein once said, "The more I learn, the more I realize I don't know." Our principle, "Learn Something New Every Day and Share It with the Team" encourages us to read broadly and study topics that pertain to our career. The more we foster a culture of learning, the more we discover how little we know as individuals and as a company. This self-awareness drives more curiosity to learn and grow.

Nobody likes to work with or for a "know-it-all."[11] A know-it-all is defined as "one who claims to know everything; who disdains advice." Both definitions describe a mindset of haughtiness and pride rather than humility.

In a franchise system we seek to attract coachable leaders. Someone who is a know-it-all does not make a good franchise partner, business leader, or team member. The power of franchising is in the sharing of knowledge through peer-to-peer sharing, as well

---

11   *Merriam-Webster* website, s.v. "know-it-all," http://www.merriam-webster.com /dictionary/know-it-all.

as training and ongoing coaching. If someone is not coachable, the power of franchising is weakened. Humility keeps us from getting defensive when people offer alternatives or disagree with us. A humble mindset invites and appreciates feedback and coaching. Humility allows us to process, consider, and, where applicable, use ideas we get from others.

We keep challenging ourselves to learn and to improve. We realize and can openly discuss our strengths and weaknesses. We acknowledge and take responsibility for our failures. Being teachable frees us from the burden of always having to be right. Every person and every situation we encounter can teach us something if we are open and receptive. Humility is a prerequisite if we are going to fully embrace the next principle, because it keeps us teachable. Humility keeps us from the dangerous belief that we have "arrived"; it keeps us intellectually hungry.

LEARN SOMETHING NEW EVERY DAY AND SHARE IT WITH THE TEAM

A CULTURE OF CONTINUOUS IMPROVEMENT

At Sunshine Brands we work hard at being a "continuous improvement company." We are always looking for ways to do it better. We know we are a good company, and we try to do things at a world-class level, but we know we are not perfect. We make mistakes every day. In today's ever-changing business environment, often described as paddling in "permanent white-water,"[12] continual learning at both the personal and organizational level is a requirement for growth and

---

12　The term "permanent whitewater" was coined by Peter B. Vaill in his book *Managing as a Performing Art: New Ideas for a World of Chaotic Change* (San Francisco: Jossey-Bass, 1989).

survival. Improvements in knowledge, competency, and skill level cannot be an afterthought—they need to be a way of life. With the current rate of change in the world today it is easy to become irrelevant and outdated within just a few years. No matter what degrees or diplomas you may have achieved in the past, if you aren't continually learning, you will become extinct. The competitive advantage always goes to those who upgrade their systems, skills, and knowledge.

We need to ask ourselves every night before we go to bed, "Was I better today than yesterday?" Learning something new day by day, step by step is the only way to improve. Consider pro athletes. They do not master their sport overnight. By the time we see them on the sports highlights, they have put in thousands of hours of practice.

With dedication, desire, and focus we can become exceptional at what we do. We all have the potential and the calling to become world-class in our field! We can all make the choice to avoid the well-worn path to mediocrity. We can take control of our own destiny and avoid the pitfalls of blame and victimization, in which a lack of skill or success is blamed on the economy, the competition, or the people we work with. Always remember, while one person is looking for an excuse, there is someone else busy finding a way to do it. We are not solely products of our nature or heredity, nor are we merely products of our nurture or upbringing; we are also products of the choices that we make. Continuous improvement is a choice. I've seen people raised in a functional family setting do nothing with their advantage. I have also met people who had suffered through a terribly dysfunctional upbringing use their struggles to build an incredible life!

"The illiterate of the twenty-first century will not be those who cannot read and write but those who cannot learn, unlearn, and relearn."

—Alvin Toffler, author of *Future Shock* and *The Third Wave*

To become a successful habit, learning requires two preconditions: one, a strong desire to learn on the part of the team member; and two, a strong supportive "learning" culture at the organizational level. Learners are open and receptive to new opportunities. Let's take a look at nine ways we learn, both as people and as organizations.

1. WE LEARN FROM CUSTOMER FEEDBACK

One of the best ways to learn something new is to listen to your customers. At each of our brands we solicit feedback from customers every month. We ask four simple questions and ask for comments. This approach is summarized in Fred Reichheld's book *The Ultimate Question.* The questions we ask to uncover our own "Net Promoter Score" are as follows:

On a scale of 0–10, with 0 being the worst and 10 being the best:

1. How would you rate the courtesy and professionalism of the person who answered your service request?
2. How would you rate the courtesy and professionalism of the service technicians?
3. How would you rate the overall value of the service provided?
4. How likely would you be to recommend The Grounds Guys to your friends and family?

The data obtained provide us with valuable feedback on our service. A low score says the customer is not happy. In these cases we need to respond immediately to the customer and understand the details of the problem. If we are open to learning, we will be able to determine whether the issue is specific to this one particular customer or if it is a more widespread problem. A mediocre score, in the six or seven range, tells us that our customer is satisfied but not necessarily thrilled or "wowed" by our service. In these cases we discuss with the team ways that we can create a more remarkable experience. A high score tells us that we have been successful in delighting our customer and that we may take the opportunity to ask them for a recommendation or referral.

The comments section also provides valuable insight into specific opportunities for service improvement. Sometimes it means just doing more of the same. Our system notifies us immediately upon receiving feedback so that we can respond to it. We listen to what our customers are saying, discuss it with the team, and then make the appropriate adjustments to our service delivery. In any case, we always take customer feedback as a gift and as a great source of learning.

2. WE LEARN FROM OUR MISTAKES AND THE MISTAKES OF OTHERS

One the most effective ways of learning is from the mistakes we make or through observing the mistakes of others. Winston Churchill said, "Those who fail to learn from history are doomed to repeat it." Mistakes will happen in any continuous improvement culture where team members are constantly challenging the status quo. Mistakes that occur due to pushing the boundaries of innovation need to be seen as opportunities and encouraged; mistakes that occur due to laziness or sloppiness are another matter altogether. In our culture it's okay to make mistakes. If you're not failing every now and then, you're probably not advancing. It's okay to make mistakes—just not the same ones over and over again.

> "Learn from the mistakes of others. You can't live long enough to make them all yourself."
>
> —Eleanor Roosevelt

The business-format franchising model is based on this principle. Essentially, when you are granted a franchise license, you are accessing all of the systems that were developed from the mistakes made by the developers of the prototype. We developed our operating system at Sunshine Brands over the years by learning from our mistakes. Every time we lost a customer or a we lost money, we asked ourselves, "What can we learn from this and what system needs to be in place to prevent this from ever happening again?"

3. WE LEARN BY READING

All of the current wisdom of the world has been written and documented. Whether in e-books, bound volumes, audiobooks, Wikipedia, blogs, or Google, there is a wealth of knowledge available to anyone who is willing to invest some time in reading. We all lead busy lives, and reading can often take a backseat. A great time to read can be while you are traveling. Instead of watching a movie on a flight, use the time to read. The commute to work is also a great time to listen to an audiobook. Instead of starting your day by filling your mind with the negativity of the daily newscast, why not feed your mind with something positive and educational? If you work in your vehicle, you have an even greater opportunity to take advantage of audiobooks. If you work out on a treadmill or a bike, then use the time to listen to an inspirational or educational book. Most smartphones today allow you to easily purchase audiobooks on demand from sites like audible.com or iTunes, making it easier than ever to carry your learning with you. In the words of Mark Twain, "Those who don't read are no better off than those who can't."

4. WE LEARN FROM PEER-TO-PEER INTERACTION

Peers are people in the same or a similar industry as you. Networking with them is a great way to learn and grow professionally. Once again, the franchise model lends itself well to this type of learning, because each of your peers are in the same business but are not in competition with you. The larger your network of trusted peers and the more often you ask questions of them, the more you will learn. Chances are that there is someone out there who has experienced the same challenges that you are experiencing—maybe someone who has already found a solution! Talk to them. Ask for their advice and guidance. Usually all you have to do is ask. I believe most people appreciate the opportunity to help others. A well-timed conference call or annual conference serves this purpose well. Speaking of which . . .

5. WE LEARN FROM COURSES AND CONFERENCES

For almost every field of work there is a professional organization that conducts an annual conference. I have gained a lot of benefit and learning by attending conferences. These are usually several days of intense learning, often described as being like drinking from a fire hose. With proper preparation and planning, these conferences can be a great source of learning.

A typical conference consists of a mix of classroom lectures, keynote speeches, and roundtable discussions, all of which provide incredible learning opportunities. Always review the conference program in advance and select the topics you feel would be most valuable. Be prepared for long, intensive days, and always try to get lots of sleep each night. This will keep your mind alert and receptive.

Conferences often require travelling to another city and can be costly, so it is prudent to plan well in advance. It is also a best practice to send only those team members to a conference who have taken full advantage of all of the free learning sources like webinars, books from the company library, and peer-to-peer learning. In our experience, only those who have already demonstrated a robust appetite for learning will truly get the full benefit from the conference. You can always tell who is at a conference because they want to be and those who are there because they were told to go. The latter are usually sitting at the back of the class, arriving late and leaving early.

We have a practice where anyone attending a conference will take notes during the sessions. From those notes they will get three new items or "take-homes" that they learned that apply to their area of responsibility. These items will be shared with the team in a debriefing meeting when they return. The team looks for ways in which to implement the newly learned information. This leads us to the next method of learning: by teaching.

6. WE LEARN BY TEACHING (SHARE IT WITH THE TEAM)

The second part of this principle is "Share it with the team." Articulating something you have recently learned to others helps to reinforce and imprint the knowledge in your own mind. The act of teaching also helps you identify areas where you need to do more research.

To integrate learning into the culture of your team, encourage team members to share what they have learned on a regular basis. We do this through the use of an internal social platform as well as regular meetings. Even if the subject matter is not directly related to everyone in attendance, it is still a good practice for two reasons: one, it creates a formal opportunity for team members to practice teaching; and two, it is always good for team members to broaden their area of knowledge, so the right hand knows what the left hand is doing. At Sunshine Brands the training programs are designed so that team members first learn the material themselves and then train their replacements, before they advance.

7. WE LEARN BY OBSERVING AND ASKING QUESTIONS

I recently met with a franchise partner who was doing some fairly complex mechanical work on a tractor. I asked him if he had mechanical background or training. He said, "I learned to do it by watching my dad. Every time I have someone do something for me, I work with them and observe what they are doing, and I ask a lot of questions. I don't do anything unless I'm learning or teaching." Now, that's a great attitude.

Our competitors aren't likely to offer up the trade secrets that they feel give them the competitive advantage, but they can be a great source of learning if we keep our eyes and ears open. Learn from the best, including great companies in other industries.

Earlier this year I had the privilege to tour the John Deere production facility in Raleigh, NC, with a group of The Grounds Guys franchise partners. Although manufacturing is a lot different from service, we were able to learn all kinds of new things. I received inspiration and value by watching the way they worked together as a team and how they managed efficiency and quality control.

Don't be afraid to ask lots of questions if you don't understand or you need clarification. I missed out on a lot of learning opportunities before I learned that the only dumb question is the one you don't ask. I used to think that asking for an explanation or for clarification would make me look uninformed, so I kept quiet. Then by observing some of the most intelligent and successful people I know, I noticed that they were the ones asking all of the questions. They didn't look uninformed or stupid; they looked engaged and intellectually curious. They were learning.

8. WE LEARN BY DOING

I started working in the tree and shrub care business fresh out of college. I had the diploma and years of "book learning" in my head. I could answer most questions that customers asked me, but I felt a lack of confidence. Once I began to apply what I had learned in class, I began to gain experience and, over time, confidence.

I remember a client who had a large hedge of overgrown lilacs lining her 500-foot-long driveway. These lilacs had not been pruned in years and were no longer blooming vibrantly. They were also blocking the views from the house. She wanted me to prune them back to half their current size. She also wanted them to produce more showy blooms.

From my college training I was able to tell her that both of these objectives could be met, but it wouldn't be until the spring after the pruning job that the lilac hedge would bloom. This was a large estate, and this hedge was an integral part of the landscape. I made my recommendations based on what I had learned in school. Externally I tried to speak with an air of confidence; inside however, I had my fingers crossed that what I had been taught was correct and that I had remembered it properly.

With every shrub I cut in half, I felt I was doing the same to the future of my young business career. The next spring, I received an ecstatic call from my customer, asking me to come over and take a look at the hedge. Sure enough, it had responded to the crown reduction and was in full, vibrant bloom. It was at that moment that I truly felt confident in applying the knowledge I'd learned.

9. WE LEARN THROUGH COACHING

Working with a coach is another great way to learn. All world-class athletes have coaches who work with them on a regular basis to help them master their sport. In the business world, coaches are once removed from your day-to-day operations, and as such provide a view of your business from a different perspective. Someone who is not involved in the day-to-day operations can see things that you may not see or provide a perspective that you may not have thought of. Coaches also inspire and motivate you when you are struggling by reconnecting you with your goals and aspirations. Lastly, a coach provides enormous benefit by holding your feet to the fire.

MASTERY

Mastery is defined as " full command or understanding of a subject, outstanding skill; expertise."[13] It may be possible to survive at the

---

13   *Collins English Dictionary* Online, s.v. "mastery," www.collinsdictionary.com /dictionary/english/mastery.

lower levels of your industry with mediocre people, equipment, technology, and leadership. In fact many companies remain mediocre for life, and they seem to do okay. But if you come up against world-class competition, you are going to need to perform at a world-class level with world-class people. This requires mastery.

> "Mastery is a mindset: It requires the capacity to see your abilities not as finite, but as infinitely improvable."
>
> —Daniel H. Pink, author of *Drive*

Mastery is also a motivator. Once people form the learning habit, several things begin to happen. One, they begin to realize how little they know; and two, they awaken within themselves the desire to learn more and to get better at what they do. This is not obsession; this is the fulfillment that comes from realizing their potential. We are born with a natural drive to be the best at what we do and to use our talents to their full potential. Over time, however, we often let this drive fade away. Perhaps others tell us that we don't have potential, and we believe it. Perhaps this is a story that we also tell ourselves. Thoughts turn into beliefs. These limiting beliefs turn into actions and become a self-fulfilling prophecy. We stop trying to be great at anything and settle into the comfort zone of mediocrity. "Don't rock the boat, do things as they've always been done, put in an honest day at work, and then forget about it" becomes our mantra.

I see work differently. I see it as a platform that challenges me to push myself farther and harder to become the very best I can be. It is an opportunity to stretch the boundaries of my potential and to inspire others to do the same. Work provides me with the chance to discover and uncover my latent talents and to use them to help make the world a better place.

The following is an excerpt from the book *A Return to Love* by Marianne Williamson, published by HarperCollins in 1992.

It is our light not our darkness that most frightens us. Our deepest fear is not that we are inadequate. Our deepest fear is that we are powerful beyond measure. We ask ourselves, who am I to be brilliant, gorgeous, talented, and fabulous? Actually, who are you not to be? You are a child of God. Your playing small does not serve the world. There's nothing enlightened about shrinking so that other people won't feel insecure around you. We were born to make manifest the glory of God that is within us. It's not just in some of us; it's in everyone. And as we let our own light shine, we unconsciously give other people permission to do the same. As we are liberated from our own fear, our presence automatically liberates others.

I watched a documentary called *Jiro Dreams of Sushi*. The film follows Jiro Ono, eighty-five-year-old sushi master and owner of Michelin three-star restaurant Sukiyabashi Jiro, as he continuously strives to perfect the art of sushi. Not only has Jiro Ono long achieved financial success through becoming one of the best sushi chefs in the world, but he has also found happiness in striving for mastery of his craft. Here is one of my favorite quotes from the movie: "I do the same thing over and over, improving bit by bit. There is always a yearning to achieve more. I'll continue to climb, trying to reach the top, but no one knows where the top is."

THE BENEFITS OF A LEARNING CULTURE

The proper application of this principle and its successful integration into your organization's culture will have a lasting and positive effect. Some of the benefits that we have experienced from a learning culture are

- Efficiency—Team Members look for ways to do things better, faster, and more effectively!

- Quality service—Improved quality of products and services.

- Confidence and competency—Higher levels of certification, resulting in increased confidence and competence. Greater trust from customers, resulting in increased sales.

- Openness to change—Increased adaptability and greater speed in learning, providing a competitive advantage.

- An engaged and inspired team—Team members who freely apply their knowledge and who are engaged in their work at the highest level.

Part 3

RESPECT

"When we treat people merely as they are, they will remain as they are. When we treat them as if they were what they should be, they will become what they should be." —THOMAS S. MONSON

BE ETHICAL AND TRUSTWORTHY IN YOUR DEALINGS
A CULTURE OF TRUST

Trust is the glue that holds an organization together. Without trust, the growth and development of a company slows to a crawl and can eventually stop. In a small organization, "The Boss" feels she cannot trust her employees, so she finds herself making all of the decisions and doing all of the important jobs. She follows up on everything and supervises as much as possible. "Nobody makes any decisions around here without first checking with me," she insists. This management style can lead to problems.

In my dealings with many small companies over the years I have heard the same challenges over and over again. "I can't find trustworthy people! I would love to free up my time to do other things, but I can't trust anyone to do this job properly but me!" Or, "I've tried it before; I brought on a team and let them go at it, but they messed it up. It hurt my reputation and it cost me money! Because of this bad experience, I have gone back to the way it was before, where nobody does anything without checking with me first."

These examples illustrate a concept that we will explore further, one that I call the two ditches on either side of the road to trust. The first is the kind and free approach that can result in disorganization, confusion, and the eventual unraveling of team dynamics. The other side is a tough, command-and-control approach that can result in the eventual disempowerment and alienation of your workforce. In larger organizations, layers of bureaucracy begin to take over, stifling creativity and slowing the company's ability to execute. All of this causes trustworthy team members to feel restricted and disrespected. CARE Leadership presents a better way that is both kinder and tougher.

It is difficult to grow an organization without the ability to entrust certain tasks and roles to others. However, it is irresponsible to trust someone with an important task if they are not trustworthy. In this chapter we are going to explore trustworthiness and how to develop it within our team, our organizations, and ourselves.

Trustworthiness is the byproduct of two components. At Sunshine Brands we strive to exemplify both components by being "principled and productive." Colin Powell, retired four-star general of the US Army and former secretary of state, describes these two components as "character and competence." Jack Welch, former CEO of General Electric, looks for "values and results" within his team. Jim Collins, author of *Good to Great*, describes trustworthiness as the ability to "preserve the core and stimulate progress." Warren Buffett, CEO of Berkshire Hathaway, only hires people with "integrity and intelligence." All of these essentially describe the same two components of trustworthiness. One without the other is insufficient. They are both sides of the same "trustworthiness" coin.

THE TRUSTWORTHINESS COIN

One side of the coin is character, which is defined as "moral or ethical strength."[14] On the other side is competence, defined as "possession of required skill, knowledge, qualification, or capacity."[15] If you have a team member with a great attitude and a strong desire to learn how to drive a truck but who has never driven a truck before, would you trust him to jump into the driver's seat? What about a team member who has driven for years but has a reputation for speeding, driving aggressively, and cursing at other drivers on the road? Would you trust her with your truck and your reputation?

It is important to understand this two-part trustworthiness concept. I've heard business builders say, "I hired really nice people, but when I got them on the job, they couldn't handle it." The point is not to look for "nice" people; the point is to find "principled" people who can produce or be trained to be productive at high levels of competency.

RECRUITMENT

A question I often hear is, "Do we find trustworthy people, or do we need to develop them?" The answer to that question is that you need to do both. If you begin recruiting well in advance of the need to hire, you can take your time to look for the perfect candidate: someone

---

14 *The Free Dictionary*, s.v. "character," http://www.thefreedictionary.com/character.

15 Dictionary.com, s.v. "competence," http://www.dictionary.reference.com/browse/competence.

who is highly skilled, open to learning new things, and who truly lives by your principles and values. However, there is a good chance that this person is already gainfully employed. Recruiting him or her away from their current job would certainly be desirable but may not be practical or affordable.

In most cases it is better to recruit someone who you feel can be developed into the perfect addition to your team. One candidate may be strong in character but lacking in skills, while another comes with years of experience but lacks a predisposition to the values and principles of your organization. Which do you focus on first: character or competency?

At Sunshine Brands we use the phrase, "hire for attitude, train for skill." We believe that, in most cases, if the person has the right attitude they will develop the skills required for the job quickly and easily. It is easier to impart a new skill to someone with a great attitude than it is to instill a great attitude into someone who has spent years developing a bad one. It can be done, but will require a lot of effort that could be used building your organization. Inviting a bad attitude onto your team can also threaten your entire culture. The skills that the candidate brings to the table may fill a competency gap in the short term, but the negative attitude will create significant problems down the road.

As a rule, we find people who fit our culture first, then we immerse them into our culture of learning and train them in the skills required until they have developed trustworthiness. Their desire to learn something new every day and to take ownership of their tasks will be of more value to the organization in the long run.

The higher the skill level required for the job, the more emphasis you must place on competency. I had the privilege of interviewing CFL Hall of Fame running back and former head coach of the Toronto Argonauts, Michael "Pinball" Clemons, at our company's 2012 reunion. I asked him what football scouts look for when recruiting. He explained, "In order to win championships in football, you need to start with the best players in the world. In a professional sport setting we recruit 'talent' and then go to work on their attitude." This is the opposite approach taken for hiring for most general labor positions, but in the sports arena it makes a lot of sense. Even with a great attitude and years of training, few players make it to the pros. Of course, if you had the two most talented players in the world, one with a good attitude and one with a bad attitude, the choice would be easy.

> "Mistrust doubles the cost of doing business."
> —John Whitney, Columbia Business School

As the skill requirements increase, the time dedicated to recruiting the right candidate also increases. In these situations, only invite people to the interview with the required skills and experience, and then look for the culture fit. Never hurry, and never compromise.

Once you have built a great culture and a winning team, the power of word-of-mouth kicks in, and you begin to attract great people who are both principled and productive. This should be every leader's goal.

When I hear someone say, "I don't trust my people," what I really hear is this: "I hire people without sound principles, and I don't bother to invest the time required to train them properly." Don't let this be you. Building trustworthiness is your responsibility.

TO TRUST

I believe that trusting someone enough to allow them the right degree of autonomy within your organization is one of the highest forms of human motivation. Having someone extend trust to you or extending trust to someone on your team can inspire trustworthiness. If you recall my own experiences from chapter one, I truly "found my voice" when I was entrusted with a high level of responsibility and given the autonomy to "own" my job. When you believe in a principled and productive team member (even if they don't yet believe in themselves), you help unleash their full potential.

THE ROAD TO TRUST

As leaders we need to be aware of the two ditches on either side of the road to trust. One ditch is trusting everything and everyone without proper due diligence. The other is trusting no one but yourself. Ronald Reagan is famous for the following statement that I think sums up the middle road pretty well: "Trust and verify." Whether these natural tendencies to extend or withhold trust are built into our DNA or just developed over time through experiences, we each have a natural propensity towards one or the other. In either case, it is better to follow proper procedure when extending trust in business.

The ditch on the other side of the road is the "Boss" mentality that is still predominant in many businesses. This way of thinking says, "I must retain command and control of everything." In this culture, an employee feels powerless. She can only follow orders. If employees take initiative and come up with a good plan or idea, the boss usually shuts it down or changes it to something more in line with his style. Over time the employee stops taking initiative and resorts to waiting for instructions. The "Boss" gives the orders, dictates the methods, creates the plans, and controls every movement.

When something goes wrong or doesn't work, the employee says, "I did what you told me and it didn't work—what now, Boss?" The boss, on the other hand, usually blames the employee for lack of competence or lack of common sense, not realizing that it is her "Boss" mentality that has created this disengaged, disempowered employee. The boss becomes frustrated and starts to take it out on the employees. Behind the scenes, employees complain, "If she only listened to us, she could save so much time and money; but since she won't, I'm just going to do exactly what I'm told. I don't care anymore. It's her money that she's wasting, not mine." Have you ever heard this attitude before? Have you ever worked at a place where this was the predominant culture?

I had an acquaintance who used to work on an assembly line in a car plant in Detroit. He was responsible for installing some rubber hoses and clamps into the frame of the vehicle before it passed on to the next station. It was difficult to get the job done in the time allotted, and occasionally the line was slowed down. He came up with an idea to apply a little dish soap and water to the hoses to help lubricate them and speed up the job. One day he thought he'd give it a try. He brought a small pail from home and a little brush, added a little water and soap, and brought it out to the assembly line. It worked great. He was able to increase the speed and ease of the job at his station. When he told his line boss, however, he was told, "Just keep doing it the way we've always done it. I don't have the authority to make changes to the procedures here." This was a source of frustration for him. Over time, the culture crushed his ingenuity, and he succumbed to the attitude of "just keep doing things the way we've always done them." What a loss!

Many companies have a similar culture. Innovation is slow, productivity is weak, quality suffers, and employee turnover is high. Contrast that with the CARE Leadership approach, where team members are taught the underlying principles and are then encouraged, empowered, and incentivized to look for ways to do it better. If you are not naturally the trusting type, it is important for you to step aside and relinquish control to your competent team. This can be very scary for a leader and is usually the point at which leadership development breaks down.

However, if you find yourself in the other ditch, where you extend trust without first doing your due diligence, your business can also suffer. Your team members may be happy and feel empowered at first but will grow disenfranchised with the lack of structure and the weight of responsibility they are not ready to bear. They may have great character but haven't been trained to do the job properly. When things go wrong, they unfairly inherit the blame. Alternatively, they may have the skills but lack the character to operate within your value system. They may be hitting their numbers and getting the job done but at what cost to team morale and brand reputation?

Recall Principle Three: "Don't Just Do It—Own It!" where we discussed the steps to proper delegation: demonstrate, observe, and solo. These three steps must be thoroughly completed in order to build competency in any given job.

Along with these steps of proper delegation, a leader must also set out the guidelines or boundaries within which a new leader can operate. These boundaries may be structural (systems, workflow, roles and responsibilities or job descriptions) or they can be market-driven (time-constraints, budgets or minimum requirements). In either case, these boundaries must be clearly understood by everyone.

There must also be explicit clarity on the expectations and desired results. If both parties have different ideas of what a "job well done" means, it can cause all kinds of problems and an eventual loss of trust.

As competency increases, the boundaries in which the leader can operate expand. Team members can be entrusted with more stewardship and given more responsibility. Customers extend you more trust and present you with more opportunities.

What happens now? You need to get out of the way and watch your competent, trustworthy team work their magic! Your role as a leader now changes to an assistance role, where your job is to make sure the new leader has all of the resources needed and is free of any barriers that would hinder him from being successful. In my experience, the best way to inspire trustworthiness in your team member is to trust them.

TO BE TRUSTED

Trusting your team is only half of the equation. You as a leader need to be trusted by your team, your customers, and your community. Let's explore some ways in which trust can be earned.

Trust Is Earned by Keeping Your Word

Our strategic partner, The Dwyer Group, and their associates live by a value that states, "We live our code of values by making only agreements we are willing, able, and intend to keep." This is critical to building trust. Every time we break a commitment, either willfully or through negligence, we begin to erode the level of trust in a relationship. There are times when keeping a promise becomes impossible for reasons beyond our control. The Dwyer Group handles those unavoidable situations with a value that emphasizes timely communication so as not to break trust. They say, "We live our code of values by communicating any potentially broken agreements at the first possible opportunity to all parties concerned." What a great way to operate a business, a family, or any organization!

Trust Is Earned by Being Honest

Honesty is defined as "uprightness and fairness; truthfulness, sincerity, or frankness; freedom from deceit or fraud."[16] Your parents

---

16 Dictionary.com, s.v. "honesty," http://dictionary.reference.com/browse/honesty.

taught you to be honest as a child and not to lie. They extended more trust to you when you told the truth, no matter the consequences. The temptation as a child was to "gloss over" or completely withhold the truth in order to avoid the consequences. The same temptation faces us every day in a business setting, whether we are involved in the financial inner workings of the company or we are a new hire with few responsibilities.

To be an effective leader, you must internalize your principles. Leaders directly impact whether honesty and integrity are promoted or eroded in a business culture. Cutting corners or being dishonest (even in small ways) demonstrates to your team that this behavior is okay. Every day we are faced with decisions that test our commitment to ethical business practices. For example:

- Do I pay the full license fee for the software, or do I just install another copy?

- Do I take home these supplies from work, or go and buy my own?

- Do I take credit for a team member's idea, or do I give credit where credit is due?

- Do I maximize my efforts for the company while on the clock, or do I steal a few hours to daydream or conduct personal business?

- Do I accept this cash job, and if I do, do I record it?

Often these decisions involve money. There is a concept in the study of economics known as *Homo Economicus*, or the "Economic Man."[17] It states that, by nature, people are generally selfishly driven

---

17   John Kells Ingram, *A History of Political Economy* (1888)

by one overriding ambition: to minimize cost for themselves as consumers and to maximize financial gain as a producer. Controlling spending and increasing sales is a sound approach and necessary for business success. But this cannot be your only business philosophy (a business can go off track if it is not guided by conscience). In a company where moral and ethical standards are weak or absent, the principle of the "economic man" takes precedence. For these organizations, minimizing cost and maximizing gain becomes the dominant or, in some cases, the only principle guiding the decision-making process. From time to time, business leaders will be faced with making a decision where doing what is ethical will cost them money. If maximizing gain and minimizing cost is our only principle, then ethics are put aside. Over time the desire for economic gain begins to supersede the desire for a clear conscience. Enron and WorldCom are infamous examples of companies that started out okay but lost their way because their only core value was the maximization of profit for their shareholders.

Trust Is Earned by Being Transparent

Transparency is needed in a trusting culture. Whether confronting difficult situations or dealing with more pleasant topics, it is best to be transparent and open with your team. Hiding information or having hidden agendas leads to distrust and secrecy. The more informed your team is about the realities of the business, the more secure they will feel and the more they can contribute to its success. Of course there are requirements for privacy of certain information, but we believe it is better to err on the side of full disclosure than to be too secretive and closed. Again, The Dwyer Group is a great example of this openness and transparency. I had the privilege of attending one of their monthly budget meetings at their corporate head offices in Waco, Texas. What impressed me was how a multimillion-dollar company could be so open and forthright with their more than 200 associates. They discussed financial targets and reviewed their progress. The result of this open and honest communication is a feeling of mutual trust and improved synergy within the team.

THE TOXIC CULTURE OF "PROFIT BEFORE ETHICS"

Managers who operate on a profit-before-ethics philosophy usually assume that everyone else does, too. They impose strict procedures and policies. Normal checks and balances turn into restrictive chokeholds. A culture of suspicion takes over, and morale suffers. Good, honest people are chased away by a demoralizing culture where they are scrutinized, checked up on, and watched over like common criminals. Those who remain are the ones who have learned to game the system and profit from the loopholes.

In such an environment, *perceived loyalty* becomes more sought after than honesty. Everyone is suspected of cheating or being incompetent in his or her work. People become suspicious of each other and begin to report their surmises to those in authority. More controls are put in place. Questions are asked about every conversation overheard or piece of paper left unattended. People become closed and install locks on their drawers and tighter passwords on their computers. Team members become afraid to come up with new ideas for fear of rocking the boat and arousing the negative assumptions of the "Boss." Team members who find themselves in these types of toxic cultures either seek employment elsewhere or succumb to the philosophy of the boss, where the shame is not in doing wrong, but in getting caught.

It is important to take a good look at the reward and incentive programs in your organization. Are they perhaps contributing to a low trust environment? Typical reward and incentive programs often reward only those who "hit the numbers." These programs can have little or no consideration for how those goals are achieved. Such one-sided incentive programs must be balanced with an ethics component, or they will unwittingly encourage unethical behaviors. They can even work as a disincentive toward making the tough ethical decisions. Even companies that put a lot of value in honesty and ethics find it difficult to instill those values when there is a lack of congruity between their values and their systems.

Over time it becomes easier for people to justify dishonesty in the name of the noble pursuit of financial gain. "They don't pay me enough," "I work harder than anyone else," or "I'm the boss, I deserve a few perks" become the justification.

THE BENEFITS OF A CULTURE OF TRUST

Studies show[18] that a trusting workplace increases the level of team member ingenuity, engagement, and productivity. It also encourages open communication, where people feel secure in sharing their ideas without fear of having them stolen by superiors or shot down by peers. This secure environment leads to increased innovation within an organization, giving the company a distinct advantage in the marketplace. This internal trustworthiness also helps to create corporate trustworthiness, which results in increased sales and customer loyalty.

Trust Creates Corporate Agility

In a high-trust environment, deals can be completed in much less time and for much less cost than otherwise. In his very compelling book

---

18   Source: 2002 Gallup poll on employee engagement in the workplace, available at http://businessjournal.gallup.com/content/829/gallup-study-finds-many-employees-doubt-ethics-corporate-leaders.aspx

The Speed of Trust, Steven M.R. Covey relates a story of a multi-billion dollar deal where Warren Buffett, the CEO of Berkshire Hathaway, purchased McLane Distribution from Wal-Mart Corporation. After only a two-hour meeting and a firm handshake, the deal was signed. A deal of this magnitude usually takes months to complete with teams of auditors, accountants, and attorneys on the payroll. Clearly Buffet's trust in the Wal-Mart executive team as well as in Drayton McLane Jr., CEO of McLane Distribution, created a situation where both parties were able to save an enormous amount of time and money. Think of the areas in which your business would improve and accelerate if you had a dominant culture of ethics and trustworthiness.

Trust Enhances the Ability to Multiply and Increase Capacity

A leader's trust in her team allows her to delegate important tasks with the peace of mind that they will be handled properly. This frees up the leader's time to focus on leadership and business-building opportunities. As discussed in the principle "Learn something new and share it with the team," continuous learning provides managers confidence in their teams and gives customers more confidence in the company. Once we have been entrusted with greater responsibility, it is important to deliver results. Showing competency may earn us the initial trust, but only consistent performance and production will sustain it.

TRUST REQUIRES THE ABILITY TO PRODUCE RESULTS

At Sunshine Brands we focus on results, not just activity. Usually, results are the by-product of attitude, activity (character), and aptitude (competence). A positive attitude, the right type and volume of activity, and the aptitude to apply our knowledge result in high productivity.

Customers may hire us based on our sales promises and our ability to demonstrate that we can take care of their needs, but they will lose trust in us if we consistently fail to produce results. Nothing creates trust like production. In sports, a general manager or head coach can have all of the experience and knowledge in the world, but if he doesn't win games, he will likely be fired. Business is no less harsh. We earn trust through the principled and skillful application of our knowledge and talent. We produce results by maintaining a positive attitude, continuously improving our skills, and relentlessly focusing on the right amount and type of activity.

Accountability and Self-Governance

The way we create this focus on production is by having clear goals and metrics so that team members can track their own activities and measure their own results.

Let's use a sales team as an example. We know that adding new leads and reaching out to existing leads on a regular basis is an activity that results in increased sales. From experience, we know that if we speak with a specific number of leads per week we can expect a certain percentage of follow-up meetings. From those meetings we can expect to build a few relationships that will result in a sale. With all that information, we now can determine the type and volume of activities required per week, and we need an easy way to review our progress. Our daily HUDDLE is a short, stand-up, high-energy meeting where each department quickly reviews and presents their dashboards. We hold each other and ourselves accountable. The dashboard looks like a speedometer with 0 at one end and our stated objective at the other. In this case, the objective is 100 calls to customers in one week. Our progress throughout the week is visible on the dashboard for each team member to see.

This eliminates the need for a supervisor to micromanage and allows team members to govern themselves. Everyone knows the importance of meeting objectives and works as a

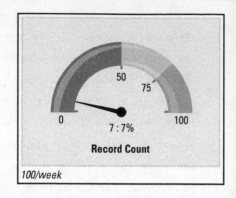

team to hold each other accountable. If a salesperson is lagging, his peers can encourage him and ask what they can do to help him reach his goals. Sometimes, what is needed is something as simple as a time block of uninterrupted calling. In this case, the whole team can cooperate to allow that to happen. This focus on attitude, aptitude, and activity produces predictable results. Building trustworthiness is our responsibility as leaders. Extending trust is a powerful motivator. Along with trust comes accountability, so work together to hold each other accountable for results. Avoid micromanagement, which flourishes in the absence of real leadership. After all, leaders hate to be managed. Be open and transparent with your team. Provide clear guidelines and objectives along with an easily accessible progress and activity dashboard. Hire for attitude, train for skill. Operate under the assumption that everybody has the potential to be exceptional. It is your job to help them find their inner genius.

"He who does not trust enough will not be trusted."

—Lao Tzo

LISTEN WELL AND COMMUNICATE WITH RESPECT
A CULTURE OF COMMUNICATION

Communication is one of the most important skills we learn in life. It is an integral part of building customer, family, and business relationships. From an early age we learn how to speak, read, write, and listen. The success of our relationships in life hinge heavily upon how well we have developed our skills in these areas.

As children we often focus on being heard. When we were hungry, we let our parents know, and they fed us. When we were unhappy about something we cried, and they took care of us. The better we became at making people understand our wants and needs, the more attention we received.

As we grow up and mature, we realize that being understood is only half of the equation. This principle starts with "Listen well," because we believe that communicating with respect starts by listening.

I came across the Chinese symbol for the verb "to listen" and found its interpretation very interesting. The left half of the symbol means, "ear," which allows us to hear. The right side, from top to bottom, means, "you," "eyes," "undivided attention," and "heart." This symbol illustrates that listening is more than just hearing. Listening well includes not just your ears, but also your eyes, your mind, and your heart.

There are some key differences between listening and listening well. The first three letters of our acronym R E S | P E C T™ pertain to listening well, and the last four concern communicating with respect. It all starts with being receptive, open, and approachable.

Receptive

Empathetic

Self-aware

Professional

Encouraging

Candid

Timely

RECEPTIVE

Listening well starts with the right attitude and the belief that there is value in everyone. As leaders we need to be open and receptive to what others have to say. If we've built a culture of trust, then people will not be afraid to share their ideas, thoughts, and feelings with us. If we have the attitude that all customer or team member feedback is a gift (whether positive or negative), we will be more approachable.

I read somewhere that Herb Kelleher, former CEO of Southwest Airlines, would answer feedback with, "Thank you. That is really helpful. Can you tell me more? Is there anyone else I should talk to?" How do people feel when they have to speak to you? Are you intimidating? Are they afraid or nervous? Or have you, like Herb Kelleher, created an atmosphere in which your team sees you as receptive to all kinds of feedback? Once you have built a reputation for being receptive and open, people will feel free to speak with you and reveal their true feelings. The next step is not just to listen but also to understand. To understand, you need to listen with empathy.

EMPATHETIC

Empathy: the ability to understand another person's circumstances, point of view, thoughts, and feelings[19]

We often jump to conclusions about what someone is telling us without really fully understanding him or her. Listening with empathy means to put yourself in the shoes of the person you are listening to

---

19   About.com, "What Is Empathy? A Definition of Empathy," http://bpd.about. com/od/glossary/g/empathy.htm.

in order to hear, see, sense, feel, and truly understand their point of view. Here are three common situations in business that require us to listen well before speaking:

1. We Listen Well before Speaking: As a Coach

A few years ago I attended a class on franchise field support. The instructor wanted to demonstrate the power of listening. As customer service reps we can feel like we need to have an answer for everything, and the instructor's point was that problems could often be solved simply by listening empathetically and by asking questions rather than answering them.

The class was divided into groups of three: a coach, an observer, and a person seeking advice. The person seeking advice confides in the coach and thoroughly explains the problem. The coach could only listen or ask open-ended questions. He was not permitted to give advice. In my group, I was the observer.

The person playing the part of the advice seeker was an executive at a large, well-known brand. She said, "Rather than making something up, I have a real-world issue that I am currently struggling with and haven't been able to solve. Maybe you can help me." She went on to explain that she and her husband were both busy executives with heavy travel schedules. They had teenage children, and she felt that they were not able to get together as a family as often as they would like.

The coach went on to ask a series of questions while listening carefully and thoughtfully to the answers. He asked questions like, "How often do you currently meet as a family? How often would you like to meet? How do your children feel about the current situation? What kinds of things do you like to do as a family when you do have time? If you were able to find a solution, who would be most affected by the change?"

As he continued to ask questions while sitting face-to-face, intently listening, I began to understand the complexity of the executive's situation. The quick and obvious solutions that had popped into my head when I first heard her challenge became irrelevant. My first thought was to say, "I have a similar situation, so let me tell you what I do," or "Why don't you try this or try that?" But in this exercise I was the observer, and even the coach was allowed only to listen and ask questions.

As she answered the questions posed by the coach, the advice seeker began to formulate solutions that she hadn't thought of before. Her eyes lit up with all of the new ideas she was discovering. As the class instructor called an end to the exercise, the executive turned to both of us with a big smile and said, "Thank you so much! That was so helpful. I think I have a solution; I can't wait to give it a try!"

I was amazed. She found a solution suitable to her problem, and all we had done was listen and ask questions. This exercise left a profound impression on me. I had been guilty of jumping to conclusions based on what I thought I'd heard, prescribing solutions based on my point of view, not the advice seeker's.

Try this approach next time you are faced with a challenging or complex situation and see what comes of it. Listening empathetically and making the effort to fully understand someone communicates that you respect and value them—and may even help them find an answer themselves.

2. We Listen Well before Speaking: When Faced with a Difference of Opinion

Often, arguments arise based on semantics (different ways of saying the same thing) or a misunderstanding of what the other person is saying. Arguments start when one or both parties place the need to be understood ahead of the need to understand the other's point of view.

However, if we slow down and focus on first understanding the point of view of the other person, we may find out that our ideas are not that far apart. In cases where there are real opposing differences of opinion, arguments serve no purpose other than to have each side dig in its heels. Listening with empathy removes animosity and communicates to the other person that you value and appreciate their opinion. This opens the door to what Steven R. Covey called "third alternative" thinking. Third alternative thinking enables people to think in terms of not just "my way" or "your way" but "could there be an even better way?" This is not a compromise where the two sides agree to meet in the middle, but rather one in which they search for a better solution that comes out of empathy, cooperation, and understanding.

3. We Listen Well before Speaking: In Sales

In the past, sales experts attempted to convince the other party that they needed their product or service. This led to the used-car salesman approach, where people were being sold something whether they needed it or not. The philosophy of the day was "grab them by the tie and choke them till they buy."

> "Trying to push your ideas without first listening to the other person is arrogance."
>
> —Michael "Pinball" Clemons

A better way is to first listen to the customer and fully understand his or her situation, needs, and wants before presenting a solution. At Sunshine Brands we use the methods taught by Jeff Thull in his book *Mastering the Complex Sale*[20] in which Jeff describes the sales process as four Ds: Discover, Diagnose, Design, and Deliver.

The process begins with discovering as much about prospects as possible before attempting to diagnose their needs. We work together with the customer to uncover their needs and the costs associated with not having our solution. If there are none, we are not afraid to walk away. Both Discover and Diagnose are exercises in listening well (asking questions and seeking to understand). Once we've listened to and fully understood the customer, we can begin to Design and Deliver a solution. Providing a lasting solution to a complex need also requires self-awareness and a full grasp of our own strengths and weaknesses as people and as a company.

SELF-AWARE

Returning to our RESPECT communications model, it's important to realize that self-awareness highlights our own capabilities, weaknesses, and perspective. It is the third component of listening well. Most often, acknowledgment of our weaknesses is the most difficult step, but it can also be the most liberating.

Self-awareness allows us to look more closely at ourselves, leading to self-acknowledgement and an understanding of our nature. It causes us to be more understanding of others. When people feel understood, they are more open and receptive to your point of view. Our own perspectives influence the way we look at a situation. Influences such as upbringing, religion, family beliefs, where you were raised, whether you were an only child or had fourteen siblings—all these help to form our perspective. The more we are aware of what

---

20   Available from Prime Resource Group: http://www.primeresource.com/

makes us tick, the more open we are to the perspective of others. It helps us to understand why others see things the way they do.

We are now ready to move to the last four letters in R E S | P E C T, focusing on communication. These include being professional, encouraging, candid, and timely. Let's begin with "professional."

PROFESSIONAL

"Watch your thoughts, for they become your words; watch your words, for they become your actions." This old saying is telling us to be mindful of how we speak. Let's look at the acronym SPEAK™ for five ways that we can communicate in a professional manner.

Sincere

Sincerity is defined as "freedom from deceit, hypocrisy, or duplicity; earnestness."[21] If you are perceived as deceitful in any way, your message will be less likely to be received.

Pragmatic

Pragmatic speech is sensible, grounded, and practical, dealing with the facts.[22] Speak about the facts and keep embellishment, analogies, and theory to a minimum.

Emotionally Mature

Keep your emotions in check and don't raise your voice when trying to make a point. When responding to emails or other digital

---

21   Dictionary.com, s.v. "sincerity," http://dictinary.reference.com/browse/sincerity.

22   *The Free Dictionary*, s.v. "pragmatic," http://www.thefreedictionary.com /pragmatic.

conversations (especially if it is an emotionally charged subject), wait several minutes before sending. Re-read the email and send only if it still makes sense.

Admirable

Keep your communication clean and free of profanity, rudeness, and off-color jokes. Political, racial, and religious jokes should be avoided. Profanity is unprofessional and contributes to a negative culture. Slander, backbiting, and gossip also contribute to the breakdown of morale and organizational unity. Speak directly to people rather than behind their backs.

> "Always respect the absent if you want to maintain the respect of those present."
>
> —Author unknown

Kinesics

Communication is only partially verbal. Kinesics is defined as the way body movements, facial expressions, and gestures serve as a form of nonverbal communication.[23] Hand gestures, smirking, smiling, and shifty or steady eyes all help to reinforce or contradict what is being said. In a conversation it is best to face other persons with an open stance, look them in the eye, and give them your undivided attention.

These five components of SPEAK will help you communicate in a respectful and professional manner and will help set the tone for a friendly, secure, uplifting, and productive work environment.

---

23   Wikipedia, http://en.wikipedia.org/wiki/Kinesics.

ENCOURAGE

The definition of the word "encourage" can serve as a job description for leadership: "To inspire with hope, courage, or confidence; hearten; to give support to; to stimulate; to spur on; to impart courage, inspiration, incentive."[24]

> "Correction does much, but encouragement does more."
>
> —Johann Wolfgang von Goethe

In my experience most people work better and produce more in an environment where they feel a sense of belonging, affirmation, recognition, and encouragement. Encouragement gives us courage to carry on when times are tough and to run even faster when things are going well. Make a continuous effort to offer uplifting words of encouragement to your team. Look for ways to recognize their efforts and let them know you appreciate them.

David Novak, CEO of YUM! Brands (the parent company of KFC), wrote in his book *Taking People with You* that he once noticed that team members were suffering under a lack of recognition for their hard work and dedication, so he implemented the "floppy chicken award." This light-hearted but meaningful award is used to recognize and encourage his team.

> "Cheer for first downs, not just touchdowns"
>
> —David Novak

---

24   The Free Dictionary, s.v. "encourage," http://www.thefreedictionary.com /encourage.

One of our team members in software development noticed that her team's day was made up of many small victories, like figuring out a new formula or learning some new code. Each of these small successes ultimately lead to the completion of the project, sometimes weeks later. She watched as team members smiled to themselves or maybe threw up a fist pump in lonely celebration.

Waiting a month for the project's completion in order to celebrate wasn't enough for this CARE Leader. She felt her team would be more encouraged and inspired if they had a way to share in these successes and support each other as they happened. She bought a maraca for everyone in the office. Now every time her team members accomplish something, they simply shake their maraca in celebration. The rest of the team will briefly pause what they are doing and shake their maracas in recognition of their colleague's success. This small effort has created a culture of recognition and encouragement. Someone may be struggling with a very complex challenge, but when they hear the maracas, they are encouraged to see their challenge through to success.

Communicating with respect means that we understand that our words and actions either tear down or build up. Despite the encouragement of others, occasionally team members can still veer off-course. In these situations it is your job as a leader to help guide them back. This may require some frank, candid, and occasionally uncomfortable conversations. Let's take a look at how candor, when seasoned with care, can show the highest level of respect to both team member and team.

CANDID

Sometimes the most caring and difficult thing you can do as a leader is to have a forthright conversation with a team member about weaknesses and shortcomings. To aid improvement, you must be willing and able to offer constructive feedback even when it is uncomfortable for you to do so. When someone is not meeting expectations or producing the required results, it is not fair to them or to the rest of the team to ignore the problem. It can be difficult to know when to be candid and when to face these tough conversations. However, if you have done your job and provided appropriate training, feedback, and support, then you are ready to have the conversation.

If you care for your team and have invested in your relationship with them, then your candid conversations will have a better chance of being received as helpful. Be aware that it may take some time for them to come to that conclusion. Candor without care can be perceived as criticism and can do more damage than good. Candor with care is analogous to a hard workout: it hurts but doesn't harm, and its intention is to make you stronger. Although "The Boss" may enjoy speaking in a blunt and critical manner, others may hesitate in having these tough conversations. It is also important to be candid in a timely fashion.

TIMELY

The final component of RESPECT is timeliness. These days we are bombarded with communications that require a rapid response: phone calls, texts, emails, external social networks, internal social networks, video calls, face-to-face conversations, and even the occasional fax. Despite the volume of conversations, it is still disrespectful to the other party to ignore or respond to them in an untimely fashion. Along with this increase in communications is a change in expectations around the meaning of the word "timely." A few years ago a response within twenty-four hours was considered timely. Today, anything less than instantaneous can be perceived as unacceptable.

Systematizing communications is a key step to improving the timeliness of your responses. Consider the following three Es of timely communication:

Expectations

Managing expectations is the first step to timely communication. There will be times when you can't respond as fast as you or they would like. For example, you can't send emails while having an important conversation, while attending a meeting, or while making a presentation. Set reasonable response time expectations to reduce frustration on either end of the conversation. If you are in the customer service business, where quick response times are critical to meeting customer expectations, you need to have a system in place for receiving and responding to those calls quickly and efficiently.

Efficiency

At Sunshine Brands we use a system where all calls and emails are captured as a CARE Ticket. Expectations are set with customers and franchise partners as to the intended response times, based on priority level. A support team member will respond to the ticket within the agreed-upon time frame. The ticket will escalate to a supervisor if left unanswered. This system enables timely and efficient communications in a professional and respectful manner. While direct access to your cell phone may first seem more personal to a customer, the feeling quickly vanishes when you are unable to answer calls because you are in meetings all day. Alternatively, you may be constantly running out of a meeting or conversation to answer calls or typing a response while nodding politely during a conversation. In both cases, conversations will suffer.

Effectiveness

Don't try to be efficient when it comes to people. You can develop efficient systems for handling the traffic and flow of customer requests, but when you engage in a conversation with people, it is more important to be effective rather than efficient. Exceptional customer support cannot have a time limit. Listening well and communicating with respect takes time, but it is worth it.

Effectiveness is a leadership skill that can be learned and improved through practice and dedication. The successful application of this principle will have a profound effect on your culture and will create an environment in which team members thrive.

In the next chapter we will look at how we can build sustainable profitability in our organizations by contributing to the triple bottom line.

CONTRIBUTE TO THE TRIPLE BOTTOM LINE
A CULTURE OF GIVING

We make a living by what we get, we make a life by what we give.
—WINSTON CHURCHILL

Everyone on our team has a responsibility to contribute to the financial viability, profitability, and success of our company. We are in business to make money, and we work hard every day to improve our bottom line. I believe in a free market where those who work hard and smart deserve to accumulate wealth for themselves. I also understand that it is unsustainable to earn financial profits in ways that do

not respect or enhance the well being
of the people we deal with, the communities we work in, and the natural
environment. The triple bottom line
stands for People—Planet—Profit
and takes into consideration our
social, economic and environmental

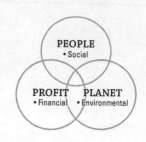

responsibilities as human beings. You don't have to choose between
"doing well" and "doing good."

In 1981 Freer Spreckley first articulated this concept when he
put forth the notion that only a triple bottom line accounts for the
real costs of doing business. Then in 1994 John Elkington, the founder
of a British consultancy called SustainAbility, coined the term "triple
bottom line."[25] The concept has grown in popularity over the years
and has given rise to what is often described as "conscious capitalism."[26] The San Francisco-based nonprofit organization Business for
Social Responsibility, which helps to measure and promote triple-bot-
tom-line companies, had only a handful of members in the '90s. Today
there are over 400, half of which are *Fortune* 500 companies!

Business by its nature can be a force for good. In a speech to
the World Economic Forum in 2008, Bill Gates pointed out that
Adam Smith, author of *The Wealth of Nations* and often cited as the
father of free-market economics, said, "It is not from the benevolence
of the butcher, the brewer, or the baker, that we expect our dinner,
but from their regard to their own interest." Gates noted that Adam
Smith also wrote the following sentence which, combined with his

<hr>

25   Tim Hindle, "Triple Bottom Line," *The Economist*, November 17, 2009, www
.economist.com/node/14301663.

26   The term "conscious capitalism" was coined by Muhammad Yunus, one of
the recipients of the 2006 Nobel Peace Prize. See http://en.wikipedia.org/wiki/
Muhammad_Yunus.

earlier statement, could be described as what some call "enlightened self-interest": "How selfish soever man may be supposed, there are evidently some principles in his nature, which interest him in the fortune of others, and render their happiness necessary to him, though he derives nothing from it except the pleasure of seeing it."

Corporate self-interest is what makes the free market work. It creates jobs and puts food on the tables and roofs over the heads of families. It sustains organizations that improve the lives of millions. Free enterprise also fosters competition that incentivizes people to innovate and create new things. In looking after its own interests, business caters to the interests and well-being of others.

But is this enough? There are always costs associated with doing business: financial, social, and ecological. Businesses reap benefits from the communities in which they operate and as such have a responsibility to contribute back to them. Businesses also create pollution while conducting their activities and have a responsibility to reduce their negative impact on the environment. If businesses were to use the power of innovation, technology, labor resources, and entrepreneurial skills to tackle some of the problems of the world, imagine the good that could be done. Businesses have the ability to participate in a positive way in the well-being of the communities in which they operate, and they don't have to wait until they are large and successful to do it. For those who still believe that the only business of business is business,[27] consider the following benefits of a triple bottom line:

- improved team morale and productivity;

- the ability to attract and retain great people;

---

27   Source: Milton Friedman (July 31, 1912–November 16, 2006), an American economist and 1976 Nobel laureate.

- positive public recognition: more genuine and effective than traditional advertising;

- brand admiration: people do business with businesses they respect and trust.

Let's take a look at our triple bottom line of People—Planet—Profits and what we feel our responsibility is to each of them.

PEOPLE

"People" pertains to both those we work with and the citizens of the communities in which we operate. "The whole-person paradigm" described in this book and the application of CARE Leadership principles helps us build a culture of CARE. When leaders treat their teams with respect, team members reciprocate to customers, to vendors, and to the public. Recall the 5 S's of inspiration: When the salary, security, and schooling needs of team members are satisfied, they start looking for opportunities to do something of significance that gives them meaning and purpose. As a company we support this desire by looking for ways to use our resources to benefit the people of our communities.

One of our biggest "People" events is "weCARE day," and it occurs on the first Friday of each November. We shut down our entire national workforce and mobilize an army of volunteers to help out at local charities, including the Ronald McDonald House Charities,[28] an

---

28   Information available at www.rmhc.com

organization that provides a home-away-from-home for families of critically ill children who are receiving treatment at a hospital.

Our teams wash windows, plant flower bulbs, install mulch, clean up the landscapes, and even cook and serve meals for the families. Originally, I named this day in memory of my sister, who passed away in November 2004. In a very moving and much appreciated spirit of CARE, friends and colleagues from all across North America joined in celebration of her life. Today it has grown into weCARE day because, as we expand internationally, I thought it important that this amazing day be shared with everyone. It can be about each volunteer's individual reason for giving; I go out on weCARE day for those I care about, and others can volunteer for anyone or any cause that is meaningful to them.

This day is one of the highlights of the year for our team members, and each year we receive inspiration from the selfless spirit of giving put forth by all of the volunteers. Visit www.weCAREday.com to see how you can get involved.

Caring isn't limited to one day, of course; it happens all the time. For example, people have been inspired to volunteer their time cleaning up street litter, doing gardening work at local charities, or participating in local food and toy drives. We have found that giving our time and resources has had as much of a positive effect on ourselves as we have had on those we are trying to help. In what way would you like to give back to your community?

PLANET

Our "planet" bottom line refers to the natural environment that sustains each and every one of us. It is the one thing that unifies all seven billion human beings. We are all temporary residents and stewards of the same small planet. I believe that we have a duty to future generations to keep the planet clean, inhabitable, and thriving. I further believe that we must always look for ways to reduce our negative impact on the environment.

In our business we make money by driving big trucks and trailers to our customers' properties to provide our services. We understand that our vehicles burn fossil fuels and emit carbon dioxide into the atmosphere. We have a responsibility to find ways to cut down on carbon emissions, and we do this through our "Clean and Green" initiatives.

Clean and Green covers a wide range of sustainability programs. They include training all drivers on proper driving habits and techniques that increase fuel economy as well as the use of bio-diesels where applicable. We work to reduce waste by recycling at each of our locations and by participating in environmental initiatives such as National Tree Day[29] and Earth Day.[30] We plant trees at local schools and community centers and speak to students to raise awareness about the importance of environmental sustainability. We use environmentally friendly alternatives to chemicals and look for ways to reduce salt usage in the winter. As a policy, when booking airline travel, we pay a small, added fee to offset the carbon emissions associated with our flight. To help reduce the energy demands of home-office activities, we installed a 12 KW solar energy system that provides clean, renewable energy to the power grid.

In 2013 we introduced a new program called Trees for Carbon

---

29   http://treecanada.ca/en/ National Tree Day, started in 1992, is aimed at maintaining a healthy environment through sustaining urban and rural forests.

30   http://www.earthday.org/ The first Earth Day was April 1970.

Reduction. With this exciting program we pledge to plant a tree seedling (using only native tree species) for every customer we have and for every new customer we acquire. We plant the tree either at the customer's property or at a reforestation site. As the tree grows it will remove carbon dioxide from the atmosphere, helping to neutralize what our vehicles emit while travelling to and servicing that property. This is a simple and easily understood initiative that allows us to "get our hands dirty" and to do some hard work to help offset our emissions.

We believe we can do more. Our commitment as a company is to continually look for and implement new ways to reduce our carbon footprint and corresponding negative impact on the environment.

PROFIT

Profit is defined in the *Oxford Dictionary* as "a financial gain, especially the difference between the amount earned and the amount spent in buying, operating, or producing something." We believe that a company has to be profitable in order to be able to achieve its mission. As they say, "No margin, no mission."

In our experience, profit is the inevitable result from the diligent application of the previous seven principles. Profit results when a company maintains and grows a list of happy and loyal customers.

Loyalty rises when customers regularly enjoy a remarkable experience with your company that is only possible when you have happy and loyal team members. The culture described in this book is "the culture of CARE," in which team members care about eliminating waste, reducing costs, and maximizing profits for their own benefit as well as for the greater good.

It has been important to us as a leadership team to substantiate our efforts in this area. Our Clean and Green and Social Responsibility efforts require measurable goals and quantifiable metrics in order to determine their effectiveness. You can't manage what you can't measure. Therefore, as an organization we have embraced the 1 percent model of corporate philanthropy and social engagement. I was first introduced to this concept in 2009 while listening to Marc Benioff, CEO and founder of Salesforce.com, who was speaking at a conference in San Francisco. Marc and his team thought that if enough companies were to donate 1 percent of their time, 1 percent of their product, and 1 percent of their equity to causes that are important to them, many of today's problems could be eliminated. Colin Powell, a good friend and mentor of Mr. Benioff, who was also speaking at the conference, had encouraged Marc to adapt the 1 percent model[31] from day one. Marc joked that at the time it was fairly easy to do, as he had no money, no product, and no time! Today however, Marc is running a multibillion-dollar company that now donates over 300,000 hours of community service, $26 million in grants as cash donations, and has over 12,000 nonprofit customers who receive free or deeply discounted services. Both Marc and Colin Powell went on to encourage as many people in the audience as possible to adopt the 1 percent model in their companies.

I was so inspired that I thought I'd give it a try. In our first year we were able to donate our time by volunteering at some great charities, but we struggled to find ways to donate our services (coaching and leadership training). To make up the difference we increased our cash donations. As it turns out however, there is a large need for leadership training amongst charitable and other nonprofit organizations, and we now donate those services. Our goal is to inspire as

---

31   For more information visit: www.sharethemodel.org

many companies within our franchise network and beyond to adopt the 1 percent model. Just imagine what a difference we can make!

> "What is the use of living, if it be not to strive for noble causes and to make this muddled world a better place for those who will live in it after we are gone? How else can we put ourselves in harmonious relation with the great verities and consolations of the infinite and the eternal? And I avow my faith that we are marching towards better days. Humanity will not be cast down. We are going on swinging bravely forward along the grand high road, and already behind the distant mountains is the promise of the sun."
>
> —Sir Winston Churchill

Part 4

ENJOY LIFE IN THE PROCESS

By living our Code of Values, we enjoy life in the process!

ENJOYING LIFE IN THE PROCESS
RANDOM ACTS OF CARE

The Culture of CARE has been the secret to our success to date and will continue to be, well into the future. It has allowed us to attract great people to our ever-growing team and to grow our brand from nothing to a multimillion-dollar, multinational service franchise. I believe that you can achieve success in your organization by understanding and applying the principles contained in this book, and I know that by doing so you will enjoy life in the process. In the final chapter of this book are stories submitted by people who have been inspired by the Culture of CARE. I hope you enjoy reading these stories as much as I do.

Treating everything and everyone with respect. Darla is an honorary team member! She lives at a health center we take CARE of. When we met her, a doctor had given her four months to live. She had lost all hope. She began to refuse her treatments and didn't want to go on with life. Our team member noticed her sitting in her room, staring out the window. He smiled to her and waved while mowing the property. She began asking her nurse to push her in her wheelchair to the window on mowing day. She looked forward to The Grounds Guys visit, and her spirits lifted and started to come back. The next week she put on makeup and asked to be pushed outside. Our team member stopped to say hi. They became friends. She asked for a gold Grounds Guys shirt, and he got her one. Now she looks forward to the weekly lawn service visit and a push around the facility. The doctor told us yesterday she is doing her treatments and progressing now! I want to publicly thank our team for caring.

[Update a year later] Darla recently passed. A family member told us that she was buried with her Bible, a Yankees cap, and her Grounds Guys shirt. When I heard the update, my heart was touched. Here is a lady I barely knew, but we were able to bless her with a small gesture of care. This was extremely humbling.   —KEN H.

Have fun and love what you do! The Grounds Guys of Owensboro planned a trip to a local theme park in June of last year. We worked really hard and serviced all our customers' needs in the first four days of the week. On Friday we spent the entire day at the park; most of the day was in the water park since it was so hot outside. We enjoyed the water slides, riding the water coasters, and relaxing in the lazy river. The best part was when the guys teamed up to dunk the boss in the wave pool. We all enjoyed some life in the process that day. —**BRAD B.**

Learn something new every day and share it with the team. Creating a wholesome, caring, and stimulating work environment for our team members is our number one priority. This focus has given us a great return on investment. We recently built a training center at our headquarters, showing our team that we are committed to learning something new every day and that we are ready to invest time, money, and effort to making them happier in their workplace and assuring them of long-term stability. We finally get it! People finish school and enter the workforce; human nature keeps them craving more education and learning. Unfortunately, we are not always afforded the opportunity to continue learning in our jobs. The Grounds Guys of Aurora will always satisfy the craving for education. Learning something new every day and sharing with our team keeps us all stimulated and engaged. More importantly, it keeps us happy and enjoying life! —**MARCO AND NATALIE R.**

Be humble. Being coachable allows us to be good coaches. The greatest leaders in this world are servants. There is an expression in Spanish that says: "el que no sirve, no sirve." Translation: The one who is not a servant achieves nothing. Living in a constant state of humility and thankfulness allows us to inspire many other people. One of the greatest accomplishments of my entire professional life has been to take my daughter Gabrielle to the Ronald McDonald House on weCARE Day. Watching her wash windows while singing her little heart out was an extraordinary experience. The icing on that special cake was to hear her thank me over and over for having this opportunity to give, to share, to love, and to care. Life has never been so fulfilling.   —ERIK P.

The Culture of CARE. The best way I can describe what the Culture of CARE means to me is to recall a scene in the movie *As Good as It Gets*. Jack Nicolson and Helen Hunt were sitting in a restaurant for dinner. After making a comment that left Helen Hunt angry she insisted that he say something nice to her. It took him a moment, but he spoke of a time when he couldn't walk out of his home and face the world without the help of his medication. "Until one day, I just stopped taking them," he said. "How is that a compliment?" she asked with a tone of sarcasm. "Don't you see?" he said, "You make me want to be a better man!" That's how I feel, working here and being part of all this; it makes me want to be a better person. Every day our Culture of CARE is injected into my day. From our energetic morning huddle that leaves me charged and ready to learn something new each day to the genuine "Thanks for a great day" from my employer as he leaves the office. It's so easy to get excited about your day when you know it's going to be better than the one before it.   —IVA C.

Don't just do it, OWN it! I want to tell a story about the principle of ownership and taking responsibility. Half of marriages today end in divorce. The purpose of this story is not to study "why" it happened, but "how" to deal with the aftermath. My ex-wife (Jennifer) and I separated in 2009. From the very first stressful day, we decided that we were going to make all our decisions with the best interests of our children first and foremost. Jennifer and I decided on collaborative law to take us through the process. After a total of one meeting, we agreed, signed, and were done. By choosing to act with our children's best interest first, we avoided all the "he said, she said" bitterness that quite often complicates divorce proceedings. Many parents do not understand the stress and anguish a child experiences during divorce. By focusing on our common goal of "the best interest of our children," we have removed our self-interests, allowing us to communicate openly and freely with respect. As a result, we have not strayed from our common defined goal(s) and enjoy a harmonious relationship with no animosity and tension. There are different ways to take ownership and responsibility. It just depends on how you handle the 10 percent of life's adversity.   —**MICHAEL M.**

As the Director of Services, I would like to tell you what happened this morning at our condo. One of our residents needed an ambulance, and considering the storm we were having, getting to the house would be a big problem. Within a couple of minutes of the ambulance arrival, The Grounds Guys' small plough was clearing out the driveway and behind the ambulance so it could back out easier. I called Dave T. and asked how this happened. He said he saw the ambulance and sent his driver over to clear the driveway. I thanked him for doing such a thoughtful act and told him how it was truly appreciated. Dave sounded very busy with this storm, but he still took his driver away from his work to help out. He needs to be recognized for this kindness. I hoped the board will keep this in mind when negotiating his new contract   —**LYNDA C.**

◈

Treating everyone and everything with respect. As a new addition to the team, we're all required to attend Training Week, whether we work for the home office or for a franchisee. During the week of training, we discussed the Culture of CARE and how it should and will impact all aspects of our lives. Even in the first couple days, that really hit home. I was on my way home one afternoon that week and decided to stop for gasoline when I saw a sign for *really* cheap gas. As I'm just starting to fill up, an old car pulls up in the stall next to mine and sits there for a few minutes with the engine running, and no one gets out. Now this isn't exactly the greatest part of town, and as a young woman, you know what you think of when it's starting to get dark out, you're alone, and someone's just sitting in their car with the engine running, next to you. When the driver finally opens the door to get out, it's an elderly man struggling with his cane and the cash in his hand en route to the convenience store to pay for his gas. I walk up to him and ask if he'd like me to run his money inside instead of making the trek himself. With the biggest smile on his face, he thanks me and hands me his cash. When I get back with his five-dollar bill in change, he offers it to me in appreciation for my help. I smile and decline the money, telling him it's just something anyone would do to help out. He shakes my hand, kisses it, and tells me, "God bless." Guess that CARE really hits home, without even thinking about it. That's why I'm so thankful to be working for a company that instills that mindset right from the beginning.   —KATIE A.

◈

Don't just do it, OWN it! One of the small things I do to allow my team to "own it" is what I call the "13-minute rule." I have told each of my staff that if a customer makes a request that seems to be outside of the scope of their work, and they feel they can get it done in thirteen minutes or less, that they have the authority to get it done. Giving people parameters like this makes them feel trusted.   —CHRIS D.

Random acts of CARE. Amazing experience today. I was driving in the truck with one of our team members and he saw an elderly lady raking leaves in her front yard in heavy winds and rain. Without hesitation he said, "We need to stop and help her." I wasn't about to argue, so we pulled over, grabbed our rakes, and helped her finish. She was so amazed that someone in our business would pull over to help expecting nothing in return. She had lost her husband of fifty years in March and we could tell it was emotional and meant a lot to her that we helped. I learned a valuable lesson about the culture of CARE from my team member today. I don't honestly know whether I would have stopped if I were alone; we had somewhere to be, and that might have seemed more important. Thanks, Bo, for living out our code of values and showing me what it means to CARE.   —KENNY S.

Random acts of CARE. Just before Christmas I was approached by the postmaster in my town. She saw me wearing my gold Grounds Guys windbreaker and, recognizing the name, came to share a story that left me feeling on top of the world. I would like to share that story with you as evidence of the code of CARE in action. When Julie and her husband came home one very snowy evening before Christmas, they were already worried about how they would help their severely disabled daughter, Jennifer, into the house. Jennifer has a lot of difficulty moving on snow-covered and icy surfaces.

They were overwhelmed with tears of joy when they saw a Grounds Guys team member clearing out their driveway and sanding/salting their walkway. "For several weeks our driveway has been cleared and walkways sanded by an anonymous helper in our area," Julie said to me. "It has meant so much to us . . . we didn't know who to thank. We all got emotional as we thought, *Wow, someone really does care.*" There is nothing more powerful than random acts of CARE. Keep up the excellent work—it makes a meaningful impact on people in our community.   —SCOTT B.

∽

Random acts of CARE. I wanted to stop and take a moment again to thank the person who stopped and helped me. After a financially hard period of being unemployed for six months as a single mom, I was headed to my first day at work. As I was getting on the freeway to drop my kids off, I had a flat tire. Crying, and stressed that I was going to lose the job I just got, at the Spokane Valley Mall, a guy pulled up behind me, came to my window, and asked if he could help.

He introduced him self as "Phillip with The Grounds Guys," and I told him there wasn't much he could do for me, since I didn't have a spare tire or any extra money. He looked at my tire and said to give him twenty minutes. Twenty minutes later he returned with a brand new tire and put it on. I asked him for his info so I could repay him, and his exact words to me were "Don't worry about it. Good luck with your new job, and hope you have a better day."

It touched my heart that a complete stranger would care so much about someone else. He truly made my day. He deserves great praise for what he did. Thanks again to Phillip.   —LINDSEY

∽

Random acts of CARE. No good deed should go unnoticed. That's why we want to thank The Grounds Guys of Paducah, Kentucky.

Recently one of our team members' vehicles quit working in the middle of a busy intersection. While she awaited help from our office, some gentlemen from The Grounds Guys pulled over, ran from their truck, and pushed her car out of the road.

We're so appreciative of their help!   —ANONYMOUS

Random acts of CARE. Hello. I want to write you a quick note to commend and thank two of your team members for an amazing gesture of kindness and goodwill.

I'm a deputy sheriff at the Josephine County Sheriff's Office in Grants Pass, Oregon. On Friday, July 19, I was dispatched to Upper River Road, a busy rural roadway, for a report of a traffic hazard. A box apparently fell out or off of an automobile, and it contained a lot of glass and other items. One entire lane was covered with broken pieces of glass of various sizes. My responsibility was to slow and redirect traffic until a public works crew could arrive with a broom to sweep the debris out of the road and prevent flat tires or traffic crashes. As I waited, I was kicking large pieces of glass out of the roadway as numerous cars passed by, some at a high rate of speed.

One of your trucks with two men in it passed by me only to return a few minutes later. These two employees of yours stopped and retrieved a flat shovel, broom, and wheelbarrow from the truck and proceeded to sweep the debris out of the roadway. In a time where most people are selfishly in a hurry everywhere they go, it was an awesome gesture of kindness for these two men to stop and help me render the roadway safe. I want you to know that I will recommend your company to anyone who asks about landscape services because these men proved to me that they really do care.

I'm having a hard time expressing my gratitude for these two awesome guys but please know that these two men are doing a great job of representing your company in a positive, friendly, and caring way. Please let these gentlemen know that their act of kindness did not go unnoticed and that I'm extremely appreciative.

—DEPUTY S.

∼

Random acts of CARE. Over a week ago, on a late Friday afternoon, my vehicle died on a busy street near an intersection in Barrie. People were in a hurry to start their weekend and gave dirty looks and/or shouted at me as I stood there in the scorching heat with the hood up. CAA had promised to show up in one hour and fifteen minutes and two hours went by with no help in sight. It was just after the police officer told me I had to call a tow truck that a man in a truck that was marked "The Grounds Guys" stopped and asked if I was OK and if I needed help!

Your team member Bill went on to analyze my situation, gave me a boost, and made sure that I made it safe and sound by driving behind me to my home.

It is through meeting people like Bill that your belief in humanity gets renewed! Not only was Bill polite and sensitive to my predicament, but he also spoke with great pride about the company he works for and their motto of caring for people. This is why I call Bill your best ambassador ever, as you could not buy the type of advertising his good deed resulted in.

Thank you, Bill, and thank you, The Grounds Guys!

—GUDRUN G.

∽

I will continue to post random acts of CARE to my blog, www.random actsofcare.com, as I am made aware of them, so be sure to subscribe. I hope you have enjoyed this book and that you are inspired and energized. I look forward to hearing from you, and I wish you success and significance in your professional, personal, and family life.

ABOUT THE AUTHOR

With over twenty years of business success to his credit, Peter van Stralen is a certified franchise executive (CFE) and the visionary CEO of Sunshine Brands®. He is passionate about sharing the culture of CARE by teaching the principles of CARE Leadership. In his spare time he can be found fishing with his kids or conquering the local hills on his mountain bike.

SPEAKING EVENTS

To book Peter to speak at your event visit *www.petervanstralen.com.*

The CARE Leadership keynote is designed for leaders and aspiring leaders at all levels. Peter will energize and inspire your audience, leaving them equipped with practical tools and ideas that can be applied immediately.

Introducing The CARE Leadership Training Program.
Enroll today and immediately start to create a culture of CARE at your organization!
Visit www.createacultureofCARE.com for details.